WITHDRAWN

BEING JAZZ

My Life as a (Transgender) Teen

JAZZ JENNINGS

EMBER

Visit us on the Web! randomhouseteens.com
Educators and librarians, for a variety of teaching tools,
visit us at RHTeachersLibrarians.com

The Library of Congress has cataloged the hardcover edition of this work as follows:
Names: Jennings, Jazz, author.
Title: Being Jazz: my life as a (transgender teen) / Jazz Jennings.
Description: First edition. | New York: Crown, [2016]
Identifiers: LCCN 2016009206 | ISBN 978-0-399-55464-3 (hc) |
ISBN 978-0-399-55465-0 (glb) | ISBN 978-0-399-55466-7 (epub)
Subjects: LCSH: Jennings, Jazz—Juvenile literature. | Transgender youth—United States—Biography—Juvenile literature. | Transgender people—United States—Biography—Juvenile literature. | Transgender people—Identity—Juvenile literature. | Transgenderism—Juvenile literature. | Transsexualism—Juvenile literature.
Classification: LCC HQ77.8.J47 A3 2016 | DDC 306.76/80835—dc23

ISBN 978-0-399-55467-4 (pbk.)

Printed in the United States of America
10 9 8 7 6 5 4 3
First Ember Edition 2017

Random House Children's Books supports the First Amendment
and celebrates the right to read.

This book is dedicated to those kids who have lost their lives because they couldn't live as their true authentic selves, and to trans youth worldwide who are paving the way for those who follow.

It's a boy—not!

CHAPTER 1

"When is the Good Fairy going to come with her magic wand?"

When did you first know?

I get asked a lot of questions about my life, and that's the one that comes up the most. The answer is easy. Ever since I could form coherent thoughts, I knew I was a girl trapped inside a boy's body. There was never any confusion in my mind. The confusing part was why no one else could see what was wrong.

When my mom, Jeanette, got pregnant with me, she was convinced she was going to have a girl. At her baby shower, her friends all crowded around her belly and did the necklace test—that old-timey trick that's supposed to predict what kind of baby a woman is going to have. You hold a necklace with something heavy attached to it, like a pendant or a ring, over a pregnant belly, and if it swings back and forth it means she's having a boy. If it moves in a circle, a girl is supposedly on the way.

This witchy little version of a gender-test ultrasound nailed it with every single one of my mom's pregnancies. It just took a little longer for everyone to realize the fetus fairies actually got it right with me.

When Mom was pregnant with my older sister, Ari, she and my dad, Greg, had just moved to Florida so he could start his law practice. She only had a few new friends at the time, so she didn't have an official baby shower but still did the necklace test with her pals from Lamaze class. It circled around, and Mom gained a lot of weight (she tells me, mostly in her face and butt). When she got pregnant again with my twin brothers, Griffen and Sander, two years later and had an official shower, the necklace marched back and forth like a little soldier. With the boys, she barely gained any weight. No one could tell she had a bun in the oven if they looked at her from the back, which is especially weird since she had a couple of them in there!

I was a surprise. When my mom first started feeling sick less than a couple of years after the twins, she thought she had the flu. As soon as she realized what was really happening and began putting on tons of weight, she knew she was going to have another daughter even before her friends did the necklace trick for the third time in her life and it spun around in circles like crazy. Everything about the pregnancy was identical to what she had gone through with Ari, so she was completely shocked when the *official* ultrasound revealed a penis on my body.

My dad didn't really believe any of the old wives' tales that my mom was into, but he always smiled and nodded along with what she said. He's sweet like that. My parents have known each other almost their entire lives—they were neighbors growing up in upstate New York, and met when my mom was five years old and Dad was four! Their fathers were doctors who worked at the same hospital, and their mothers were good friends, but when Mom was little she just thought of my dad as the annoying kid who lived a few houses down, and she wanted nothing to do with him. As he got older he became kind of a troublemaker with a loud mouth, but he finally calmed down around age ten when his parents threatened to ship him off to military school if he didn't get his act together.

All the time my mom was ignoring him, Dad had a crush on her from afar, despite knowing they weren't each other's type. He'd sneak glances at her at the local pool, and when they were older and in high school he even loaned her his jacket one night when he saw her shivering at a soccer game.

They didn't get together until years later when Dad's brother proposed to one of Mom's friends. My mom's parents were invited to the engagement party along with Mom, and both of their mothers sat Mom and Dad down at a table to look over a photo album with pictures of the spot in Europe where the proposal had happened. One by one, everyone got up from the table and left, leaving Mom and Dad alone. Mom was impressed that he'd finally shaved off the mustache she'd never liked, and it was obvious he had been working out—he no longer looked like the scrawny kid next door. They went on their first date that very same night after the party ended, and saw *Bride of Chucky*—the fourth and most romantic installment of the *Child's Play* killer doll film franchise. The movie must have worked its magic, because they moved in together not long after. When Dad got into law school in Columbus, Ohio, Mom agreed to move there with him, but only if he proposed first. So he did!

When I finally came along seven years later, they named me Jaron—a compromise between Jordan and Aaron. Dad was pushing hard for Jordan, but my mom had once dated a guy with that name, so she shot that down. For a while they settled on Owen, but then they switched to the Jordan and Aaron combo. It was conveniently gender neutral, which would come in very handy down the road.

As I began to grow, my family thought my obsessive interest in girly things was just a normal developmental phase. I have really strong memories of the emotions I felt before I could speak, as well as my actions—I figured out how to undo the snaps on my onesie to turn it into a dress shortly after I began to walk.

Like any kid, I took a lot of baths with my brothers and sister, and I'd compare my genitals to theirs. My little penis felt so wrong on me. I wished I could take the sponge and wipe it off, and behind it I'd magically find a "gagina" like what my sister and my mom had. It definitely bothered me, but I remember feeling frustrated and confused more than anything else. It was a strange growth hanging off me that didn't look at all like it belonged there.

When I finally did start to talk, I'd say "dwess like Awee" to my mom every time she put clothes on me. She misunderstood, thinking I was trying to show off my independence and letting her know that I could dress myself just like my older sister did.

I get why she would have assumed that at first. I was an extremely self-reliant toddler. Here's a good example of just how in control I liked to be: At night, I slept with a pair of blankets, each covered with the same Noah's Ark print of animals marching two by two. I liked to keep my temperature perfectly regulated while I slept, so I'd cover up with one blanket and keep the other by my side. I'd wake up as soon as I got too warm and immediately switch the covers, pulling the cooler one over me, the way most people flip their pillow on a hot summer night. I'd continue switching the blankets all night long, barely waking myself up in the process. I wasn't going to settle for anything less than what made me the most comfortable. And during the day, what made me comfortable was wearing a dress.

Around the house, I was pretty much allowed to wear whatever I wanted. I'd steal Ari's oversize pink or purple T-shirts and wobble around the kitchen in dress-up heels covered in feathers. (In fact, I first started wearing those heels back when I was still in diapers.) My parents were cool about it but drew the line at going out in public dressed in girls' stuff. Mom would put me in shorts styled for boys, and I'd scream and cry as she dragged me to the car. I didn't just like girly clothing—I felt ashamed and humiliated if I had to wear anything else.

Sometimes it helps people understand the feeling better if I put it like this: Imagine a young boy who is super into trucks and cars and playing in the mud. Then imagine that every time his parents take him out in public, they parade him around in a pink frilly dress with a parasol. The humiliation he'd feel is exactly the same humiliation I felt having to wear plain shorts and a T-shirt. I couldn't understand why my parents, who were as loving and caring as anyone could hope for, would force me to go through that kind of torture.

The more words I learned, the more I started to verbalize my feelings. Whenever my mom or dad would compliment me by saying something like "Good boy," I'd immediately correct them.

"No. Good *girl*."

When I was around two years old, I had what I now refer to as the Good Fairy dream. After a long morning of playing with Ari's dolls, dressing them up and staring enviously at the smooth area between their legs, I took a nap in my sister's bed. I had no idea that I was asleep—the world seemed crystal clear as a grown woman wearing a blue gown floated into the room. She wasn't quite like the imaginary creatures you see in cartoons, but I knew instinctively that she was a fairy, thanks to her gossamer wings, the glowing light all around her, and the magic wand that suddenly appeared in her hand. Other than those fantasy details, she looked and acted like an adult, full of purpose and authority.

I don't remember her exact words, or even if she spoke out loud at all, but I knew why she was there. She promised to use her wand to turn my penis into a vagina.

I was ecstatic when I woke up. I felt like all the answers to my prayers were possible. The dream had felt so true, so real, that I knew it was just a matter of time before the fairy would appear again and do what she'd said she could do.

I ran downstairs and found my mother sitting in our living room.

"When is the Good Fairy going to come with her magic wand?" I asked.

"The who?"

"The Good Fairy, who will turn my penis into a vagina!"

My mom tells me now that this was a huge turning point for her, the first time she truly began to realize that what I was going through probably wasn't a phase. I remember being crushed when she said no fairy was going to come for me. I had been filled with so much hope when I'd woken up, and it was destroyed within a matter of minutes.

In response, I started to assert myself even more. My mom's parents, Grandma Jacky and Grandpa Jack, were visiting us from New York not long after I had the Good Fairy dream. (They've since moved down here to Florida full-time.) While I don't remember this specific moment, they tell me they were sitting in the living room when I marched down the stairs wearing a flouncy pink dress with a pink feather boa wrapped around my neck, along with my dress-up heels and loads of costume jewelry weighing down my wrists and fingers.

"My oh my," Grandpa Jack said.

Grandma Jacky tells me that I got to the bottom stair, sat down, crossed my legs like a proper little lady, and just stared at them. She says she knew it was a declaration, and that I was definitely looking for some sort of reaction as I searched their eyes for approval. For her, the realization that something was different about me came less from what I was wearing and more from the way I was sitting and my body language.

During Grandma Jacky's visits, I'd do things like put on a blond wig and a bra over my clothes while brushing my mom's hair. One day when Grandma Jacky took me shopping and she told me I could pick out a toy, I headed straight to the Barbie aisle. In my child's mind I remember it as a wall of pink that seemed to go right to the top of the ceiling and stretch the length of the store in either direction. I was allowed to pick a doll instead of the G.I. Joe figure Grandma Jacky knew I wouldn't want anyway.

That didn't stop her from trying to get me to play with boy toys. I had no idea that she'd call Ari and ask her to get me interested in toy trucks, to which Ari would reply, "Oh,

Grandma," with an eye roll practically visible through the phone. My siblings simply didn't care. They didn't get why anyone thought what I liked was a big deal.

Grandma Jacky wasn't going behind my back to be malicious. She was worried about how the world might treat me. She was also worried about my mom, who was growing more and more concerned about my behavior. Mom has a master's degree in clinical counseling, so she decided to start doing some research in her copy of the *Diagnostic and Statistical Manual of Mental Disorders* about what I was experiencing.

The DSM is a huge book that lists all the different mental conditions known to the medical world. It gets revised and updated as doctors learn more about mental health, and back then the most current version still included something called gender identity disorder. The word "disorder" has a negative connotation that's pretty offensive to transgender people. (The same manual used to list being gay as a disorder, too.)

My mom read the DSM checklist to see if I fit the criteria for this so-called disorder and kept her own tally in her head.

Does he insist that he is the other sex? *Yes.*

Does he prefer to wear girls' attire? *Yes, oh yes.*

Does he fantasize about being the other sex and cross-dress during make-believe? *All the time, YES.*

Does he have an intense desire to participate in the stereotypical games and pastimes of the opposite sex? *Yep.*

Does he have a strong preference for playmates of the other sex? *Only plays with girls, YES!*

It wasn't like Mom had never heard of someone being transgender. She had a general understanding of what it meant, as did Grandma Jacky. It had just never occurred to them that a kid could know with so much certainty at such a young age. Mom took all this information to my pediatrician, who, after giving her a pretty concerned look, recommended that we visit a child psychologist. The pediatrician gave Mom a referral, but after doing a little research, Mom discovered that the recommended psychologist didn't specialize in kids with gender identity disorder. She did manage to find a psychologist named Dr. Sheryl Brown who treated transgender adults, and who confirmed Mom's suspected diagnosis of me. But Dr. Brown didn't feel comfortable taking me on as a patient, since she had no experience treating someone as young as I was. That freaked my parents out, since it was starting to seem like *no one* had ever treated a kid my age with GID. My mom's cousin Debbie, who was a licensed mental health counselor (and would later go on to get a doctorate in counseling transgender youth because of me), finally introduced them to Dr. Marilyn Volker, a therapist who worked with both gender issues and kids.

I was three when we went in for the appointment, and I liked Dr. Marilyn right away. She had a very calm and soothing voice like Grandma Jacky's that made me feel safe.

Dr. Marilyn pulled out two stuffed dolls that looked like fake Cabbage Patch Kids you'd find on the counterfeit toy market, with an important difference—they were anatomically correct. She asked what I had between my legs, and I pointed to the penis. She then asked what I wanted, and I pointed to the vagina.

That was the first day I ever heard the word "transgender." I remember feeling this overwhelming sense of relief that there was finally a word that described me—a girl who had accidentally been born into a boy's body.

No one really knows why people are born transgender, but there are a few medical theories. The most talked-about one is that a hormonal imbalance during pregnancy might cause it. Some doctors believe it might be a brain structure thing. It's even possible that it's genetic. No one knows for sure, but whatever the reason, it's real and no one's fault.

Dr. Marilyn made sure I understood that there was nothing wrong with me. I thought everything was going to happen fast after we left, that I was finally going to be allowed to live my life publicly as a girl, but my parents still weren't quite ready to let me take the full leap into transitioning. Just because Dr. Marilyn had confirmed everything my mom already suspected didn't mean Mom and Dad immediately adjusted to our new reality. They had all the concerns any loving parents would have and were terrified about how everyone in our life was going to react, especially people at preschool. I didn't pick up on any of this at all, though. As far as I was concerned, I had been proven right, and that was all that mattered.

At home, everything was fine. I was still allowed to wear dresses around the house, and at different times I'd insist that my family call me Tiffany, Courtney, or best of all, Sparkles. Sadly, none of those names stuck, but since Jaron is so gender neutral, I'd always revert to it without being too upset that no one took my suggestions seriously.

The only problem with things going so well at home was just that—they were only going well *at home.* By the time I turned four, I began to act out, and getting me dressed to go to preschool was turning into a daily war, with me getting up early to put on one of Ari's old dresses and Mom having to pull it off me while I screamed and cried. Mom cried, too, on the phone to Grandma Jacky. Sometimes the fights and my tantrums were so bad that I ended up not even leaving the house. Something had to give.

Meet Mommy Samantha (Ema) and Daddy Jazz (Abba).
It took until the end of the year before I was allowed to
be Mommy at preschool.

CHAPTER 2

"I love you, and I love my hair!"

No matter how hard I fought, my parents weren't ready for me to socially transition in public yet. It was infuriating to me at the time, but I can appreciate now what they were going through. There wasn't any sort of transgender visibility back then. They were on a road with no map, and terrified not just of screwing me up, but of putting me in danger in a world where people wouldn't understand me.

I had been in preschool since I was two and a half and had sometimes been teased for dumb things like using pink and purple crayons when we colored, or playing with grocery carts and dolls instead of trucks and blocks. It was nothing too mean, though. I don't think children usually have a problem with what another kid plays with unless someone else has told them it's wrong or different. For the most part I was pretty friendly with everyone. The girls liked me because I liked the same stuff they did, and even though the boys sometimes made fun of me, they thought it was cool that I could get the girls to like me. Still, I rarely got invited to anyone's birthday party, which made me sad. I did have one really close friend named Samantha who I spent a lot of time with, pushing our dolls around in little plastic strollers.

Even though I wasn't allowed to dress the way I wanted at preschool, I had no problem telling the other kids what I'd learned about myself at Dr. Marilyn's office. I was too young to pronounce "transgender" correctly, so I called myself "twansdender."

Samantha and some of the other kids asked, "What does that mean?" and I said I had a girl's brain and a boy's body. I don't think they could really wrap their little heads around it, because usually the reaction was something like "Okay, let's play with the Barbies!"

I was more than happy to play with the dolls. It's strange that stuff like hair, clothes, and toys even have gender roles assigned to them, but they do. I'd clearly always been attracted to things like dolls and dresses. There are scientists who claim it might have been because that's what I saw that other girls, like my sister, Ari, were into, and that I subconsciously picked up on it as a toddler. But like I said, I've got a pretty strong memory, and I can't remember ever being remotely interested in anything else. It felt like a natural gravitational pull. My brothers had done things like paint their fingernails when they were little but had soon gone back to the types of toys and clothes and interests that boys are "supposed" to have. Like them, I was only looking to find my place in the world. And in the world of girls, that meant pink. Neon pink, pale pink, dark pink, dusty pink . . . I was *obsessed* with any object in that color spectrum, regardless of its practical use. Ari had a hot-pink Barbie music cassette that I had confiscated and carried with me everywhere for a while. My poor family had to hear the song "Think Pink" by Barbie's band Beyond Pink over and over for ages.

I loved pink so much that I had an intense reaction to a freaking toothbrush I got for Hanukkah when I was four. Cousin Debbie gave Ari a pink toothbrush in the shape of the Little Mermaid and gave me a blue one shaped like the Cat in the Hat. I was furious, not just because I hadn't gotten the pink one, but because mermaids were *my* thing. I'd been obsessed with them my entire life, and I continue to be obsessed with them even today. Someone once told my mom that it's really common for transgender kids to be into mermaids, because they don't have genitals. I guess the idea is that for trans children, having no genitals is better than having the wrong genitals. I can see the logic in that theory, but at that age all I was aware of was that mermaids were the most beautiful creatures imaginable.

Anyway, I wasn't a violent kid, but when I got that dumb blue toothbrush I hurled it across the room and ran behind the couch, sobbing my eyes out. Grandma Jacky was visiting at the time and tried to comfort me, but she was shocked at just how extreme my reaction was, since she'd never seen firsthand one of my dressing-for-school fits.

Want to hear something weird? Gender-related colors actually used to be reversed—less than one hundred years ago, boys wore pink and girls wore blue! There are a couple of theories about why the colors switched and why the color difference between genders even existed at all. Some people thought pink read more masculine, while blue felt daintier, but the idea that makes a lot of sense to me is that it was all about capitalism. Apparently department stores were the ones promoting this idea of a different color for boys and girls, as a way to get parents to shop more. If a family had a boy first and then a girl, they suddenly felt pressured to buy a whole new wardrobe instead of handing down the old clothes!

After I got permission to start dressing the way I wanted at home, my dad still wasn't 100 percent on board with what was happening. It had nothing to do with the reality of me being transgender, though. As he puts it, he thinks the universe is pretty magical and anything can happen. Based on everything he'd witnessed, me being a girl made sense to him. But he was looking at my situation through a protective lens—he was worried about how the outside world was going to react to me. Not that my mom wasn't, but Dad is more cautious by nature, and he didn't want to rush into anything. It didn't really cause any tension in their marriage or anything, but Mom was being much more active about the situation than Dad, reaching out to online support groups for advice on the best way to handle my transition, and she'd always share any information or research with him.

Those groups didn't always give her a whole lot of relief in the beginning. When she first signed into a chat forum, she asked if anyone had ever had any experience transitioning a kid before kindergarten, and got the sound of crickets chirping in return. She was desperate for some sort of manual, like a version of *What to Expect When You're Expecting* but about raising a transgender child. (Luckily that kind of book does exist now!)

Another time, a woman sent Mom a study that said 80 percent of little kids who transitioned were just gay and would transition back once they were older because they grew out of it. The study was disproven as BS, though, since none of the participants had actually ever been diagnosed with GID. (The clinic that funded that study also practiced conversion therapy to try to forcefully change a kid's natural inclinations to play with the toys they wanted to, but thankfully they recently ended the practice. Several city, state, and federal governments are now making these kinds of "therapy" illegal.)

Mom wasn't buying it anyway, even before the study was debunked. She saw how much happier I had become after meeting with Dr. Marilyn and getting permission to wear the clothes that suited me.

About a year after my first meeting with Dr. Marilyn, when it was very, very clear to my dad that I wasn't going to change, he finally agreed with Mom that it was time to let me begin fully transitioning at home. The happiness he knew it would give me helped counter his fears about society's reaction, but he wanted to get our family acclimated first, before taking that next big leap.

The first step was to tell my siblings. Dad and Mom sat my brothers and sister down to explain to them that as a family they were all going to start recognizing me for what I was—a girl. The twins, who were seven by then, took it with their usual "sure, cool" attitude, I think because they were so young. It wasn't like they were losing anything, since they'd never really thought of me as a little brother to begin with due to my lack of interest in boy stuff.

Ari took it a little harder. She really liked being the only daughter. She was nine at the time and wasn't too happy to suddenly have to share the family princess status. But after my dad explained to her that many transgender kids have really difficult lives and that more than 50 percent try to kill themselves at some point because they aren't loved and accepted, she started to cry and promised him she'd be the best big sister ever. She has been ever since, even when I'd get super annoying and copy her every move. If she got a purple hair bow, I had to have a purple hair bow, too. It got so bad that Mom would sometimes buy us matching outfits so I wouldn't be tempted to sneak things from Ari's closet. (It didn't work.) I think Ari was flattered, but I'm sure it also bugged her at times. If it did, she never let on. She's just that great.

Grandpa Jack and Grandma Jacky definitely had their concerns about how the world might treat me, but they'd witnessed so much of my behavior growing up that they knew the right thing was to go along with what made me happy.

Mom was friendly with my preschool teacher, and even though I didn't know it, they had been in constant contact. Mom let her know what I was going through, and while I still hadn't started socially transitioning by changing my pronoun and wearing dresses outside the house, the two of them were able to convince the school's director to ease up on the dress code for me. Eventually, I was allowed to wear shirts that had pictures of things like butterflies and Disney princesses. My absolute favorite was purple, with a big picture of Ariel from *The Little Mermaid* on it. The administration drew the line at these tops, though. When kids asked questions about why I could wear girly shirts, I told them it was because I was a girl. If they kept asking about it, the teacher would tell them I was allowed to be whatever I wanted to be. In the end nobody else besides me wanted to dress differently, so it didn't upset the balance too much.

Because I went to a Jewish preschool, every Friday we celebrated Shabbat. Each week, in rotation, a different boy and girl would be chosen to dress as the Ema and Abba (mother and father), sit in special chairs, and lead the class in singing a blessing over some grape juice and bread. Whenever it was my turn I couldn't stand having to be Abba because he had to wear a tie—the ultimate representation of male clothing. Both Ema and Abba wore a basic yellow smock, but Ema got to wear a necklace. It was the two objects wrapped around their necks that made all the difference—symbolic chains that advertised their gender. Even though they'd eased up on the dress code, I had to be the Abba whenever it was my turn, and I hated every second of it.

The preschool's dress code also included what you could and couldn't do with your hair. I still had to keep mine much shorter than I wanted. I tried to work around that by clipping brightly colored kids' hair extensions on, but the school's director quickly banned them for all kids, I suspected as a way of not specifically calling me out—mainly because I was the only one who got in trouble for continuing to try to sneak them into my hair. I'd get scolded, but the other girls who did the same thing wouldn't.

The kids might not have cared that much about what I was wearing, but word quickly got out to the parents, and some of them didn't take too well to it, as we found out after a playground accident.

I was climbing on the school's big green jungle gym during recess. It was one of those cool mash-ups that look like a giant took a whole bunch of different playground equipment like monkey bars, tunnels, and swings and joined them together with Krazy Glue. There were so many different fun things to do on it, including two slides. One of them was the swirly kind with a tunnel and a little house up at the top. When you were getting ready to go down, it was impossible to see if there was anyone at the bottom. It also ended with a foot-deep drop to the ground. (I know that doesn't sound like much, but remember, we're talking about preschoolers.)

I was sort of friendly with the girl who went down the slide ahead of me that day. She had a broken wrist and everyone was fascinated with her little cast. I waited for what seemed like an appropriate amount of time for her to reach the bottom and hop off, but I didn't realize she'd decided to hang out down there for a while. So when I came whooshing down, I knocked her into the mulch, where she landed broken wrist first.

There was a lot of screaming and crying and teachers running around, and the whole thing quickly got out of control. The girl told anyone who would listen that I had pushed her off the *top* of the slide, and I was expelled from recess for a week. I had to walk around the edge of the playground while everyone else got to play—a kiddie version of the prison yard shuffle. My friends all felt bad for me, and sweet Samantha even stuck by my side instead of playing with the rest of the kids for the duration of my punishment.

The worst part was that after the girl's mother complained to the school about what I had supposedly done, the director called my mom and suggested that I had pushed the girl because I was jealous that she was an "actual" girl.

As difficult (and ridiculous) as that was for Mom to hear, changing preschools wasn't really an option. Mom had already been able to make so many inroads for me, and she had a good relationship with my teacher, and the idea of having to start all over somewhere else was too much—even after Mom started hearing rumors that some of the other parents were saying they didn't think what she was allowing me to do was right. Even worse, some were saying *she* had actually wanted a little girl instead of a boy. They were gossiping that she was forcing me to believe I was a girl, when in reality it was the complete opposite—I had been the one trying to convince *her.*

The memory of Mom calling me a girl for the first time is so clear in my mind. She was sitting in her bedroom, and I walked up to her and asked if she would put my short hair into pigtails. She bunched up what little she could on both sides of my head, so that I looked like Pippi Longstocking if someone had attacked her braids with a pair of scissors. We stared into the mirror together, and Mom told me I was a very pretty little girl.

She finally understood!

"I love you," I said, looking up at her. "And I love my hair!"

I started dancing all around the room, thrilled out of my mind. But suddenly I stopped in my tracks, full of concern. Griffen and Sander had recently started teaching me how to kick a soccer ball around the backyard, and I was really having fun with that.

I looked up at Mom again and asked, "Can girls still play sports?"

"Girls can do anything they want," she answered.

My first day of kindergarten. Notice my school-ordered skort keeping everything "tucked away."

CHAPTER 3

"I have a girl brain and a boy body. I think like a girl, but I just have a boy body. It's different from you."

A dance recital finally changed everything. Our preschool didn't have a proper theater, so all of our parents were expected to squish together along the sides of the building's narrow lobby while the kids filed out of our classroom to perform a choreographed dance routine to "The Good Ship Lollipop."

I knew all the moves. It was mostly a tap routine, along with my favorite moment, when we all dropped into a split (or as close to a split as a four-year-old can handle). Something snapped, though, when I walked out and saw all those parents freaking out over the adorable little tutus and pink dresses the rest of the girls got to wear. I got *mad*.

I was wearing yellow shorts and a pink T-shirt with a

few Disney princesses on it, and when the music started I stood still and barely even tapped my big toe against the floor. I watched the girls prancing around, their dresses swishing all over the place whenever they twirled. The mothers were laughing and pointing, so excited for their pretty little daughters. Toward the end of the song I noticed that my mom was video recording me.

I stared into the camera lens and tried to pour all my anger, frustration, and sadness into it. *This is all wrong!* I screamed inside my head.

Somehow my mom heard me. She tells me now that seeing how miserable I was up there was her final wake-up call. I was surrounded by so many other girls, stuck in a body that didn't feel like it belonged to me and wearing clothes that made me visibly uncomfortable. It was a situation she'd witnessed me in a million times before, but something about the look in my eyes on that particular day convinced her that it was time for me to publicly live the way I was meant to live.

Still, they waited about six more months, until my fifth birthday, to have my coming-out party. I didn't want to wait that long, but Dad continued to be very, very cautious, wanting to move slowly and not rush anything. It worked out well, though—since we were going to have a party anyway, it got to be an extra-special occasion, and my parents didn't hold back on anything. They rented a bounce house with a water slide and a snow cone machine, which Sander and Griffen immediately announced they were going to run. (My parents found out later they were charging everyone $5 per treat and pocketing all the cash!)

On that day, I was finally allowed to wear whatever I wanted in front of my friends and their families because Mom had invited my entire preschool class. By that point I'd collected a pretty huge girly wardrobe by sneaking Ari's old clothes out of her bedroom, and since it was a pool party I narrowed down my choices to two different brightly colored one-piece bathing suits that no longer fit my sister. One had rainbow stripes with an almost metallic, sparkly sheen all over it, and the other one was tie-dyed. Of course, I chose the sparkly option! I felt like it was the one that best represented me. Not that I was using words like "represent" back then. It was more like I grabbed it and yelled, "MINE! MINE! MINE!"

It was the happiest day of the first five years of my life. There was no nervousness or fear about how people might react. I couldn't stop smiling because everyone would finally see my real, authentic self in such a beautiful bathing suit. My parents were allowing me to be the girl I knew I was. None of the kids from school reacted at all. I think by that point they were just used to me. I remember seeing a couple of moms giving me funny looks, but I didn't care at all. Nothing was going to bring me down that day. Except for the moment when I broke a piñata and the other kids rushed in and took all the candy before I could get any— *that* part sucked!

The next big step in my social transition was going

out in public dressed like a girl. We waited for the school's holiday break, and my parents decided Disney World would be a good place to start, since it was nearby and so packed with all kinds of people that no one was going to be looking out for a kid dressed in a way they didn't agree with. I'm sure no one would have noticed, but Mom and Dad wanted to make sure I was completely free of scrutiny. I mean, what could go wrong at the Happiest Place on Earth?

Mom took me to Target to buy a bunch of girl clothes for the trip, but my favorite outfit was a long pink dress with Tinker Bell on it that I stole from Ari. My hair was still short but starting to grow out, and it was long enough that Mom could pull it up into two proper pigtails on either side of my head.

Still feeling protective, Dad was a little wary of my outfits, but nobody glanced at me twice during our entire trip, except for one time when we were in line for a ride and Ari forgot to use the right pronoun. I had fallen behind a little and Mom asked where I was. Ari saw me a few feet away and said, "He's right there," before correcting herself. I got a few weird looks, but I think mostly everyone thought it was Ari's mistake. Which it actually was!

The Disney trip was different from my birthday party because it lasted a couple of days. I was out in the world as myself, not in the safety of my house and backyard. And no one thought there was anything different or strange about me. When preschool started back up again, I still wasn't allowed to wear a skirt, but I was allowed to start growing my hair out and wear tops that were much more feminine and sparkly than the Disney princess shirts I'd worn before. Sometimes Mom would volunteer at school, and once a boy approached and asked why I dressed the way I did.

"You know how some people want to be a daddy when they grow up?" Mom said. "Well, Jaron wants to be a mommy."

She figured it was the easiest way for someone as young as this kid to grasp it. The boy just stared at her before wandering off.

The one time I was able to get away with wearing a full-on dress to preschool was for Dads' Night—a costume party for the kids and their fathers.

Dad continued to be less than 100 percent comfortable with seeing me wear girls' clothing at the time, but I still hadn't picked up on it, probably because I was so happy and he hid it well. He was slowly adjusting to my transition, which is normal for any parent, but his nervousness didn't stop him from letting me dress up in a gown for the party. All the little boys wore superhero costumes like Spider-Man and Batman, while many of the girls went as princesses. (I was Belle from *Beauty and the Beast*!)

It had been one thing for Dad to see me dressed in the clothing I wanted to wear on our home turf or in a crowd of strangers. The costume party was made up of all the same kids who had been at our house on my birthday, but that evening they were with their fathers, while at my party they had come mostly with their moms. It helped Dad that my mom was there that night, too, volunteering as the official yearbook photographer, because he knew she could keep an eye out for any trouble. He didn't need to worry, though. The dads were all cool, even though he could sense that they were having a tough time grasping the situation. Many years later, he told me that night was a big turning point for him. He saw how happy I was dancing in my princess dress and suddenly stopped caring what the other men thought. He was all in. I was his daughter, I was happy, and that was all that mattered.

At first I was only allowed to wear dresses outside the house on the weekends, and Ari would take me to the girls' bathroom with her whenever I needed to go. But toward the end of the year even the preschool began to fully acknowledge who I was—by finally letting me be the Ema on Shabbat!

I didn't know it at the time, but my mom had been doing a lot of behind-the-scenes work to learn as much as she could about being transgender. This was the first year she attended the Philadelphia Trans-Health Conference (it's exactly what it sounds like), and it ended up becoming a huge part of our lives later on. During my mom's first trip, she attended a workshop and asked a ton of questions about raising a transgender kid. No one there had any experience with it, so they ended up adding her to the panel and asking *her* a ton of questions!

She talked to everyone about what she and Dad were

currently working on—the process of enrolling me in kin-dergarten as a girl. Mom knew that the principal at our local school, Ms. Reynolds, was super conservative, but she'd seemed nice every time Mom had met her over the previous six years, since my brothers and sister already went there. I'd even met Ms. Reynolds in the lobby of the school one day when we were there to pick up my siblings. My hair was almost to the bottom of my ears by then, but I was wearing overalls, so I looked pretty boyish. Ms. Reyn-olds had smiled down at me and asked what I wanted to be when I grew up.

"Everything!" I answered.

To head off any issues from the beginning, Mom tried to set up a meeting with Ms. Reynolds to explain my situ-ation before kindergarten started. After promising to con-tact the school board and get back to Mom, Ms. Reynolds ignored all her follow-up calls. It became so obvious that she was blowing off my parents, and they were at a loss about what to do. That's when they had the very smart idea that maybe a little media attention might speed up the process. If the administration wasn't going to listen to us, my parents decided to take a risk and see if they'd listen to a journalist who could address the issue in a larger way.

They contacted the local paper and worked out an agreement where a reporter could do a story about the problem they were having getting me enrolled as a girl, as long as the paper didn't name the school, used fake names for all of us, and didn't show our faces. The plan worked! The article got a lot of attention, and a week after it came out Mom got a call from Ms. Reynolds, who invited her in for a meeting, all the while saying she'd never gotten any of the other messages.

Mom went in there prepared. She brought my dad, as well as another lawyer, who specialized in LGBT civil rights, and Dr. Marilyn. Ms. Reynolds listened to what they all had to say.

She didn't exactly get it.

At first, her concession was that I could enter school as "gender neutral" and be an "it." My mom compared the idea to them thinking of me as being more like Elmo from *Sesame Street* than an actual person. My parents were not having any of that, so they continued to push back. The meeting dragged on for several hours, and eventually they wore Ms. Reynolds down and she agreed to let me enter kindergarten as female. I was still going by Jaron at the time—I kept that name all through elementary school, except for when media coverage started happening later on—so we didn't have to file any official name change paperwork.

Like preschool, the elementary school had a dress code, and Ms. Reynolds insisted that I wear either pants or shorts. My parents fought back some more and were able to get her to compromise with skorts—skirts with shorts underneath them. With a skort, if you have a boy body, everything down there stays tucked away. The problem is that skorts aren't made for boy bodies, which presented a big issue that I'll explain in a sec.

The main thing that Ms. Reynolds wouldn't budge on, no matter what, was the bathroom. I would not be allowed to use the girls' room under any condition. I had two options. First, I could use a unisex bathroom in the classroom, where everyone could hear me pee. Plus there was no lock on it, so anyone could walk right in on me, which happened a lot until I decided to stop using it. My other option was the bathroom in the nurse's office, which was used for sick kids to puke in more than anything else. Not to mention that I usually had to wade through several bleeding and crying children to get to it.

My parents weren't going to let the issue slide, but they figured as long as there was somewhere I could go for the time being, they could keep fighting while I officially started school as a girl.

Since my preschool had been on the other side of town, I was now entering a world where no one had ever thought of me as being a boy. It was like the whole slate of my life had been wiped clean and I was getting the chance to start over as the real me. The Good Fairy still hadn't come along with her magic wand, but entering a new school as a girl was a nice start toward that dream promise being fulfilled.

On my first day of kindergarten, the school mysteriously went into lockdown, which meant no one was allowed on school property except for the kids. Parents had to drop their children off along the side of the building, where teachers escorted everyone inside. Parents of kinder-gartners were allowed in, but we were all rounded up in the cafeteria for a while before class, like in a holding pen, instead of getting the chance to go right into the classroom and meet the teacher.

Mom had never seen anything like it before and couldn't figure out why the teachers were acting so strange. She suspected it might have something to do with me, but when she asked, she was told it didn't. She later found out through teachers she became friendly with that the ad-ministration had been scared the media was going to show up because of me, even though the newspaper article had never specifically mentioned our school. Nobody came, though—thank God. That was the last thing anyone in my family wanted.

I made two friends right off the bat on the first day—Rebecca and Catherine. I loved that there were girls who wanted to be my friend simply because I was a girl, too. My preschool friend Samantha and I were still close, even though we were now at different schools, but she still hadn't quite gotten the hang of my correct pronoun. There was no way Rebecca and Catherine would ever slip up and call me he, because they had no idea that I had ever had to present myself as a boy.

That's not to say kindergarten was perfect. Remember those skorts I mentioned? I kept getting in trouble because I was always picking at myself down there, trying to arrange my penis into a comfortable position. Which was basically impossible. My teacher was very sweet and accommodating of my situation, but she'd still have to constantly rush over to my chair and lean down to whisper at me to remove my hand from my pants. My teacher understood why I kept doing it and didn't want to send me to the principal's office, but she also didn't want to keep calling me out in a way that would draw attention from the other students. She talked to my mom, and together they came up with the code phrase "Jaron, stop bothering yourself" to get me to remove my hands from my skort. With the number of times she had to tell me, it's not surprising that I soon became obsessed with drawing explicit body parts in school.

This ended up being a good thing, because my artistic side was really firing up for the first time. I'd always been into drawing, but I suddenly found myself constantly sketching during class. And what I was sketching was fairly realistic portraits of vaginas, breasts, and butts. All the boobs were big because my mom's were, and since those were the only ones I'd ever seen naked, they were all I really knew.

Anyway, I was drawing what was on my mind, what I wished I had.

My teacher sent me to Ms. Reynolds's office one day when she caught me with one of my "nude pics." Ms. Reynolds had no idea what to do about it except call my mom, who grew scared that the principal was going to use this seemingly deviant behavior as an excuse to tell her that allowing me to transition was wrong. Ms. Reynolds didn't go quite that far, but Mom definitely felt like she was the one in trouble. "These kinds of drawings are utterly unacceptable and inappropriate," Ms. Reynolds told Mom, before warning her that she'd better figure out a way to make me quit.

Mom was able to convince me to stop sketching at school, and ultimately I never got into any real trouble. For the rest of the year, I was kept in check via our teacher's behavior monitoring system. In the front of our classroom, she hung a big picture of a traffic light, with the red, yellow, and green lights all equally bright. The green light had a smiley face on it, the yellow light had a face with a straight line for a mouth, and the red had a frowny face. Each student in the class was represented by a different little clip with our names on them, and based on how we behaved, the teacher would move each kid's clip up or down the traffic light.

Well-behaved kids landed on happy green. If you'd been a little bit bad you got the straight-line yellow face, and badly behaved kids stood out at the top, next to frowny red. My clip usually stayed put at red. I liked to talk a lot, even when we were supposed to be working, and I would get up out of my seat and wander around. I think I was just so excited at being out in the world as a girl that it was hard to sit still. After my trip to the principal's office, the teacher moved my clip so high up that it wasn't even on the image of the traffic light anymore. My perfectionist tendencies hadn't emerged yet, so I didn't really care.

That spring, Mom took me with her to the Philadelphia Trans-Health Conference, which she'd gone to the year before, and I guess technically you could say that was the first time I ever spoke on a panel. The truth is that I was running around with my new friend I'd met there: Stephanie, a trans girl who had been adopted from China. I was sort of aware that Mom was talking at the front of the big conference room, and I heard my name mentioned so I ran up to her, totally unfazed by the roomful of people staring.

"Oh, here she is! Do you want to say hi to everyone?" Mom asked.

"Hi," I said.

"Do you want to tell everyone how you feel about being a girl?"

"I'm happy. I love who I am! Can I go play with Stephanie now?"

I obviously got better at public speaking as I grew older, but I don't think that was such a bad start!

At school I became more and more confident and even told a few kids, including Rebecca and Catherine, that I was a girl who had been born in a boy's body. Nobody believed me then. They thought I was just being weird and would shut me down by saying, "Yeah right, Jaron." So I stopped mentioning it.

I had no idea that during that whole school year my parents were being majorly pursued by television producers from New York City, who wanted nothing more than to hear me talk about how I'd been mistakenly born in a boy's body.

Barbara Walters, Ari, and me. My interview with Barbara Walters, which was my first public declaration that I am a girl, was groundbreaking for the world.

CHAPTER 4

"I think what matters most is what a person is like inside."

The local newspaper story about me that my parents had used to land a meeting with Ms. Reynolds ended up getting picked up by the *Village Voice* in New York, where a representative from the TV newsmagazine show *20/20* saw it. She reached out to my parents to try to convince our family to appear on the show, and Mom and Dad immediately said no.

You've got to hand it to the people in charge of the show—they didn't give up and worked on my parents for ten full months. Mom and Dad's worries were 100 percent legit. They wanted to protect me, because some larger news outlets like CNN and the *Miami Herald* had also picked up the article, and conservative talk show hosts like Glenn

Beck were making mean comments about our family on the air. Mr. Beck said that letting me go to school as a girl could be considered "borderline child abuse," when in reality it was the exact opposite. For some weird reason he also decided that I must be a kid who eats paste.

I had no clue any of this was going on, but my dad's secretary was telling him things like "Um, I've got Barbara Walters on line one for you."

Some producers flew down to Florida to meet with us, and then flew my parents and me to New York to meet with Barbara Walters and some *20/20* executives and more producers. Dad was against doing the show for a long time, but Mom started to get a gut feeling that as long as our privacy was protected, my story might help other kids. I was happy and adjusting to my new life so well that she thought we might inspire other families who were going through a similar situation. She'd spent so much time on the support message boards that she knew there wasn't a lot of information for parents out there, and there was definitely no visibility of kids like me. She would have done anything to have had a resource to turn to when I first started to exhibit signs of being transgender.

That's the whole reason why about halfway through kindergarten, Mom and Dad founded a public charity called TransKids Purple Rainbow Foundation. Their main goals were to educate schools and communities about trans youth and to raise money for different trans charity groups. (They started it with another mom of a transgender kid, but she later dropped out because her child decided she didn't want to be in the public eye.) I knew the foundation existed, but I was still too young to be very involved, even though my parents graciously named me an honorary co-founder.

When Mom and Dad finally sat me down to ask what I thought about doing the television show and explained how it could help other transgender children, I immediately said yes. I wish I could say that my intentions at the time were all about being an advocate, but I was in kindergarten. I wanted to be on TV! I thought I would be famous! I didn't understand how important doing the show really was. I'd had such a great experience with my family that I thought I was just like anybody else. I was happy living my life, and I assumed everyone else was, too. I didn't feel a strong need to search out and make other transgender friends because I already had friends who didn't think there was anything wrong with me.

After some more negotiating, my parents finally came to an agreement with Barbara Walters and the producers that everyone was comfortable with. In the beginning, Dad had wanted all our faces to be blurred out, but the producers convinced him that it was important to put real faces to the story so the viewers could better empathize. Mom and Dad decided to let the producers shoot inside our actual house, the idea being that if the audience could see inside our home and get a glimpse of how normal and loving our day-to-day life was, it might open people's hearts more.

Our family's name would be changed, and Dad came up with Jennings, sort of in honor of news anchor Peter Jennings, but also because it's a pretty common last name. Mom and Dad both used fake first names, and I got to pick my own. I went with Jazz, which was a name I'd always loved after watching Ari play Princess Jasmine in the school play version of *Aladdin*. I was also still kind of into the name Sparkles, but Jazz won out. Just imagine, in some parallel universe I might be going by Sparkles Jennings right now.

The other rules my parents put in place were that the show would only be aired once, to better ensure our privacy, and that where we lived would not be mentioned. Most important in my eyes now, they also insisted that the show not offer any kind of counterpoint, like talking to some whacked-out doctor who might say that being transgender was all in my head. There was no way they were going to introduce my story to the world if it had to go up against that kind of ignorance.

The day before the interview, I drew a picture of Barbara Walters to give to her when she came to our house. My parents sat me down and explained how the whole thing would work, that Barbara was just going to ask me things like "When did you first know you were a girl?"

I was like, *I got this*. But I became nervous once the whole crew showed up. All those people running around with their cameras and lights and giant foam-covered microphones overwhelmed me. When Barbara finally arrived at the house I was shocked, because she was wearing the exact same outfit I'd drawn her in the day before! Black pants with a pink blouse. The coincidence helped make her seem more like a normal person. It felt like she was my friend and not some big important celebrity news lady.

When I watch the video now I think I act shy, like any six-year-old with a bunch of cameras in their face would. It didn't take very long for me to feel at ease with Barbara, though.

When Mom was going over with me what was going to happen during the interview, she also suggested that maybe I sing something if I ended up feeling comfortable enough. I had recently started going to an acting school with Ari called Broadway Bound, and we'd put on a production of Rodgers & Hammerstein's *Cinderella*. Ari played the Fairy Godmother, and I'd landed the very important role of Mouse #4. During rehearsals, I would sit in the audience and memorize the lyrics to all the songs. My favorite was "In My Own Little Corner." It didn't hold any special meaning for me at the time; I just thought the melody was so pretty. I would sing it at the top of my lungs whenever I was in the tub.

After Barbara and I sat and talked in my bedroom for a while, I got used to everyone being there and agreed to sing, even though I was getting over a cold and my voice was all raspy:

In my own little corner in my own little chair
I can be whoever I want to be
On the wings of my fancy
I can fly anywhere
And the world will open its arms to me

I didn't get how profound the lyrics were for my situation until I was much older and watched the show again online. It's a song about the desire to become your authentic self and have everyone accept you for the person you are. I even got up and walked over to an actual *little chair in the corner* to sing.

When the special aired in April 2007, it didn't have any big effect on my life. One kid in school was like, "I saw you on TV!" And that was only because she'd happened to wander into her living room while her parents were watching. She saw my face and then walked out. It's not like five-year-olds are begging to watch *20/20*.

The show wasn't anything huge in my mind, but it turned out that it was affecting other children's lives. Mom and Dad started to get tons of thank-you letters from parents of transgender kids—these families no longer felt alone in what they were going through. We managed to achieve the original goals of both educating people and sending out a message of comfort and normalcy.

Overall, things were going pretty great at the time, except for one major deal—I wasn't allowed to play girls' sports. And I loved sports.

I just want to play soccer with the other girls.

CHAPTER 5

"You can't tell me who I am. Because you don't know what's going on in my head or how I feel, and you can't define me. I define me."

I'm going to be skipping ahead in time here, since the saga of me being allowed to play soccer on a girls' team started in kindergarten but ended up becoming a years-long battle.

Ever since I could walk, Griffen and Sander liked playing sports with me, and I loved playing with them. Playing ball didn't take time away from my mermaid dolls. Like it was for millions of girls, being into sports was just another part of my personality. We'd spend hours kicking a soccer ball against the side of the house, and when I was a little older we'd shoot hoops in the driveway. We always had fun together, except for the times when they'd let me score extra points on purpose and then I'd brag about how good I was.

I didn't have to steal points from my brothers for very long, though. I *was* good, especially at soccer. We had a full-size soccer goal net in our yard, and the twins taught me how to place my shots in order to score. I was a natural at getting the ball to go anywhere I wanted with my feet, and we'd gather kids from around the neighborhood to practice and play with us in an empty lot next to our house.

I joined my first team when I started kindergarten. It was a recreational league, or rec, which means you don't have to try out—anybody can play. The team was in a neighboring town, and since it was coed, I could play as myself and no one noticed or cared. We were called the Flagstar team, and my official team picture was taken at the beginning of the school year when my hair was still growing out. In it I'm kneeling, grinning from ear to ear, totally unaware that my shirt has buckled in the wind so that it reads FAGSTAR. Ugh.

I lost my first tooth right before the first game, and I took that as a good omen. It felt symbolic, like a sign from above that I was growing into a new part of my life.

Playing on a team of mostly strangers (Samantha was on the team with me, too) instead of just with my brothers threw me off a little at first, and I wasn't that great. But I steadily got better and better, and by the end of the season I could score two goals in a single game. The next year, I signed up for an all-girls team in our hometown. I had to be registered in the rec system to prove my age, and my parents needed to show my birth certificate. The rec team organizers weren't even checking for proof of gender, but just in case, Mom conveniently placed an "accidental" coffee ring over the little box with an "M" in it, obscuring the letter. When Dad slid the document across the counter for the clerk to check my name and age, he also placed his thumb over it for good measure, and it worked! I was registered as a girl.

All my soccer practice began to pay off in gym class at school. I started getting picked first for teams, and I was proud that I could beat a lot of the boys. I played on the rec team again in second grade, and we didn't have to show my birth certificate again, since I was already in the system. By the spring I was dominating on the field, so we knew it was time to move on to the big leagues—travel soccer.

Travel is different from rec in that you have to actually try out to get on a team. It's much more competitive. I tried out and won a spot, and since we were nearing the end of the season, I joined as an unregistered guest player. But we needed to officially register me before the next season started the following year, when I'd be in third grade, and my parents decided to tell my new coach that I was transgender. She didn't care at all—she just loved having me on the team!

When my parents first began the registration process for the travel team, they turned in a clean version of my birth certificate, which said I was male, along with letters from my physician and Dr. Marilyn that explained I was transgender. While they waited to hear back from the state soccer association for confirmation that I could play, I was only allowed to practice and play in a few local scrimmages. It killed me to have to sit on the sidelines during the actual games. I wanted to be out there supporting my teammates!

By the time the third-grade season started, I was denied a female player card, and the state soccer association ruled that I wasn't allowed to play on any girls' teams. But my parents didn't tell me, and to try to beat the system, my coach kept me on as an unregistered guest player. I didn't know I was going against regulations and thought everything was just fine. During our first tournament, I made a goal by kicking the ball from the complete opposite end of the field! (Well, it wasn't a full regulation-size field, but it was still cool!) While my mom was standing up cheering she overheard one of the other coaches say, "I'd take that girl on my team any day!"

My parents were pushing back hard against the state soccer association after my registration got denied. They immediately went to the National Center for Lesbian Rights for help. Don't let their name fool you—the NCLR fights for all LGBTQ communities when it comes to discrimination in sports. They got right to work, reaching out to other trans rights advocates like the Transgender Law & Policy Institute, to build a team of professionals who could come up with a report that supported all the reasons why a child should be allowed to play sports in their affirmed gender. The eventual outcome was a paper called Guidelines for Creating Policies for Transgender Children in Recreational Sports.

While all that was happening, I continued to play until it blew up in our faces. My team made runner-up in our division tournament, and right before the award ceremony, the state soccer association found out that I had played unregistered. We have no idea how. My coach got in serious trouble, and the team was almost disqualified.

I still had no clue that the fuss was all about me. One night I was lying on my parents' bed hanging out with them, and my dad told me very matter-of-factly what they had been up against behind the scenes the entire time. He was sympathetic, but he didn't try to sugarcoat it at all.

"They don't want you to play soccer," he said.

My initial reaction was shock, and then I started to cry. "But I love soccer," I choked out.

"I know, and we're going to keep fighting so you can play," he said.

I had turned nine by then and had been living as my authentic self for four years, but I think it was the first time I realized just how much being transgender could affect my life on a larger scale. All the conflicts we'd had until then—about my entering school as a girl, about bathroom rights—were issues we'd faced in our everyday lives, right around us. The idea that there was a statewide organization that was against me was terrifying. I'd understood in a general sense that there would probably be other problems

I'd have to face in life besides bathrooms and pronouns, but I began to feel the full weight of how much people didn't get what being transgender is. Nothing about the ban by the state soccer association made any sense to me. I was a girl, and I wanted to play on a soccer team with girls. What was so difficult to understand about that?

I knew it was because of bigotry, fear, and ignorance, but it just didn't compute. The state soccer association believed that because I had been born in a boy's body I had an unfair advantage, which was ridiculous. I was 100 percent a girl, not to mention the smallest one on the team. The reason I was good at sports was because I worked hard and practiced. It felt surreal and infuriating to be denied my rights after having come so far with my transition. The association was also concerned about parents from other teams suing them for allowing a child they perceived as the wrong gender to play against their kid.

I suddenly understood that the whole problem with my team nearly being disqualified from the division tournament had really been about me, and I'd never been so mortified. The idea of almost costing my teammates a win because of who I was crushed me, even while my parents explained in detail everything they were working on to try to fix things. I was so incredibly grateful that they had been doing so much while trying to protect me from the truth, but I knew it was time I really opened my eyes.

You have to understand that I was young. I know now with all my heart that there are transgender kids who experience far, far greater discrimination and hatred than not being able to play on a suburban sports team. I truly get how lucky I am. At the time, though, my small world was the only one I knew.

I didn't want to stop playing the sport I loved, so I ended up going back to rec soccer. Even though I was already in their system as female, we were up front with the league this time about me being transgender. They were totally accepting of me and I was allowed to play on a girls' team, which was great, but I knew my skill level was higher than that of the other kids on the rec team. I should have been playing travel. We won the championship that year 3–2 in overtime, and I scored every single one of the goals!

Not all the parents of other players saw my good qualities. Mom and Dad began to hear rumors that some of the teams we were supposed to compete against were planning to sit down on the field as a way of protesting me being on the team. The rec league stood behind us, though, and told the teams that were threatening to sit that they would forfeit the game if they did. Thankfully none of that ever happened, but we continued to hear that parents were complaining to the board. I think things might have died down if my playing abilities hadn't been that great, but I scored a lot of goals. I stood out and the complaints kept pouring in, so much so that Mom and Dad feared that a ban against me was inevitable.

They never stopped fighting for me, though. They petitioned the state soccer association over and over, but the association continued to shoot us down. When the next soccer season started up right before fourth grade, my dad thought it would be a good idea for me to go back to playing travel while the clash dragged on, so I could keep up my momentum and not have to face the humiliation of an outright ban from the rec board. That meant my only choice was to play on a boys' team.

He was able to find a local travel team that had one girl playing with the boys, but for all intents and purposes it was a boys' league. Because of the physical differences (and, in the league's mind, capabilities), girls were allowed to play with boys, but boys were not allowed to play with girls. There were a few truly coed teams out there, but they were in towns that were hours away from us.

Since there was at least one other girl on this team, my dad hoped the situation would be similar to me playing coed. But none of the other teams we would go on to play against had girls on them, and it messed with my head that suddenly the activity I loved most in my life was being ripped away from me because of a single letter on a piece of paper somewhere. It felt like the universe was playing some sort of cruel trick on me.

On the first day of practice, Mom and I walked down a long sidewalk that separated two soccer fields, girls on the right and boys on the left. One by one we watched the kids ahead of us splinter off onto the side they belonged to, running up to their teammates, slapping backs, and hugging each other. I could see some girls whispering and pointing at me, and I looked up at my mom.

"I don't want to be here," I told her.

I saw her eyes fill with tears and understood that what was happening was just as hard for her as it was for me. I knew she and my dad were doing everything they could to get me back on the right team. Dad thought it was a good idea for me to keep playing so I could stay in top form, but I could tell that my mom wasn't as convinced that this was a good idea. She was right.

Playing with the boys was awful. They were lame and always went on about how girls have cooties. I couldn't talk to them about anything I was into, like mermaids. I didn't feel the same sense of loyalty with them as I did on my old team. They were ball hogs, and I was the lone wolf. It didn't seem like any of them had my back, which is what team-work is all about. Even worse, I started to feel like I had before I'd transitioned. I was trapped in the wrong reality, forced into a gendered system I didn't belong in. I knew I was as good a player as any of the boys, but that wasn't the point. I started to lose confidence because I felt like such an outsider.

I fulfilled my commitment and finished the season, but the team was going to continue to play tournaments. My dad saw how miserable I was and let me stop playing with them after a disastrous meeting with my coach. It was supposed to be a normal one-on-one session to discuss my strengths and weaknesses on the field, but I froze up. I knew I couldn't do it anymore. All the frustration that had been building up suddenly exploded, and I began to cry. I knew that anything negative the coach had to say about my playing had nothing to do with my abilities and everything to do with the fact that I was playing on the wrong team, with the wrong people.

Dad felt terrible after that, and I could tell he was beating himself up a lot. He thought he had misguided me, but I know he was only trying to keep me active in the sport I loved while he and my mom looked for a solution. The coach ended up emailing Dad after I quit, and wrote that he wished he could build a separate team that I could play on. It was a sweet idea, but I didn't need a special team for me. I just needed to be allowed on one for girls.

My old coach on the travel team let me come back to practice with them after I tried out again, since everyone has to try out each season, but I had to sit out every single game. I hated not being able to support my teammates, and I'd watch from the bench, furious about the injustice of it all. I knew that getting angry was better than becoming depressed, but it was a tough battle in my head between the two feelings.

That January, I was issued a US passport that recognized me as female. The process was really easy—all the forms were right there on the website for us to print and take to Dr. Marilyn and my pediatrician. We were so excited and thought there was no way the state soccer association could turn me down again. My dad wrote another letter and supplied them with my new passport, my birth certificate, my Social Security card, letters from two different doctors affirming my gender, a copy of the TLPI's Guidelines report that the NCLR had helped put together, and a copy of the U.S. Department of State Foreign Affairs Manual's section on changing gender. Even the federal government, not to mention any foreign country I entered, knew I was a girl!

Nope. Rejected again.

Dad finally accepted that the state soccer association was never going to budge on their own. So Dad went over their heads to what he thought was their governing body and appealed my case directly to an organization called US Youth Soccer. They told him they agreed with the ban, but if the United States Soccer Federation (USSF) agreed to lift it, they would have to comply. So he immediately went to the USSF.

While all this was going on, I continued to practice and watch my teammates compete, as well as play with my brothers at home. I was about to abandon all hope and quit for good when it finally happened. After the USSF's independent board reviewed all the information that my dad had supplied, they stepped in and took the unprecedented action of demanding that the state soccer association issue me a female player card. They were awesome and took things even further by bringing in a member of NCLR to create a task force to write a transgender-inclusive policy to be followed by all states, so that no other transgender athlete, regardless of age, would ever have to go through what I had. Now if only all other sports leagues would follow their lead!

I couldn't believe that by fighting so hard for me, my parents ended up helping to make a change that affected the entire nation. I'd already started to speak on some panels with my mom and do more interviews about my life and transgender rights, but this was the first time I saw just how much good advocacy work could really do. I was only eleven, but it made me want to start working even harder.

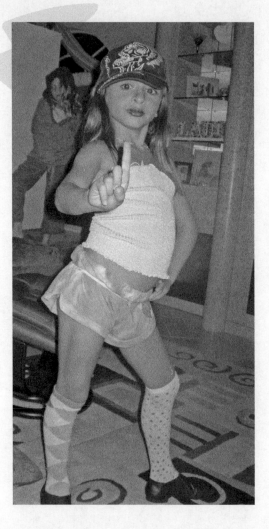

I might not have been a star at Next Stop Broadway, but I loved to dress up and ham it up at home and with my friends.

CHAPTER 6

"I share my story so that my message of loving yourself and knowing that it's okay to be different can be spread everywhere."

My soccer battle was still ahead of me when I first transitioned in kindergarten, but for now I was feeling so confident about the world accepting me as a girl that I was ready to start exploring my dramatic side. I've always been a singer, as I tried to prove to Barbara Walters. Even today I belt out tunes at the top of my lungs in the bathroom and will suddenly burst into song midconversation with someone. That's just part of who I am. I'd already done theater camp with Ari during the school year, and the summer after kindergarten ended I decided to work even harder and attend another local theater camp called Next Stop Broadway. (They might have been setting their expectations a little high with that name.)

NSB was a day camp for kids six to thirteen, with three different sessions spread out over the summer so kids could enter and leave as they needed or wanted. Everyone was divided into groups by age, and the older kids always got the lead roles in whatever production the camp decided to go with in a particular session. That first year we put on *Grease*, and a couple of the youngest kids, including me, got to sing one line each. Mine came during the song "Look at Me, I'm Sandra Dee," and was "No, *I'm* Sandra Dee!" I made sure everyone in the audience believed it.

Ari always got lead roles. Like I said earlier, she'd be the Fairy Godmother, I'd be a mouse. She played Miss Hannigan in *Annie* at Broadway Bound, and I was some random orphan. Ari always worked with me, though, to try to help me get better parts. She'd rehearse with me at home and give me tips, like teaching me how to really project my voice out into the audience. We'd make up our own strange plays and perform them for the family and her friends on the lower half of the twins' bunk beds, using a blanket tucked into the upper mattress as our stage curtain.

Once school started again and I entered first grade, my behavior in the classroom calmed down. My new teacher also used the traffic light system, and my clip never went up to red once, maybe because I was getting to act out onstage. I went to yellow a few times, but for dumb little things like accidentally knocking my glue stick to the floor and taking too long to pick it up. I had chilled out with drawing naked pictures in school, but I still sketched them at home every now and then.

A lot of kids in my class were still learning how to read, and because I'd been reading since I was in preschool, I ended up working with the other students and became a sort of teacher's helper. Our teacher didn't know how to use the Internet very well, so I taught her how to get the best results out of her Google searches. I started getting straight As, but even more exciting for me was that I started having my first sleepovers with my friend Rebecca.

My mom knew I had told Rebecca I was transgender, but she wanted to make sure Rebecca's mom knew, too, before I was allowed to go over to their house. Mom was all about disclosure and created an unbreakable rule that I couldn't go over to anyone's home unless they knew I was trans. The same went for people who came into our house. You never know how people might react, and my safety was the most important thing to Mom. She wasn't about to put me in a situation where a seemingly normal person might freak out if they didn't know about me already.

Rebecca's family was very accepting, and I loved spending the night with her. We would build forts in her living room out of sofa cushions and sheets and watch movies while eating popcorn. In the morning her mom would make us her specialty—pancakes in a rainbow of colors, thanks to food dye.

What I liked even better than the pancakes was this one game we'd always play. Well, it was less of a game and more of a "let's pull down our pants and show each other what's there" sort of situation. We didn't waste any time by pretending we were playing doctor—it was just *schwoop*, undies down, there it is. This was totally normal little-kid behavior, and anyone who tells you different is just trying to shame you, so don't listen to them.

Anyway, I don't remember feeling jealous that Rebecca had the parts I needed. I'd seen my share of vaginas at home so I already knew I wanted one. It was definitely interesting to see a new one, but I think the game was more to satisfy Rebecca's curiosity and help her better understand me and what being transgender meant. Just because there was something different between my legs didn't make me any less of a girl in her eyes. It only strengthened our friendship.

One body-related issue that *did* make me jealous, however, was that my brothers got to run around the neighborhood with their shirts off on hot days. Now that I was officially a girl in the world's eyes, I had to keep mine on, and I thought that was one of the most unfair things I'd ever heard of. It wasn't like there was anything to show off. And besides, what happened to Mom's message of "girls can do anything"?

Mom refused to budge, though, so in a fit of rebellion I decided I would become a boy again, for the sole purpose of being able to take my shirt off outside. The next morning I wore an Under Armour shirt that I stole from Griffen to school, and got a ton of funny looks. I felt utterly ridiculous and scrapped Project Boy in less than twenty-four hours, resigning myself to a life of being too hot when I went out-side. There are worse fates.

By the time I was enjoying first grade, the *20/20* episode had gotten so much attention all over the world that my parents were flooded with more interview requests from people like Tyra Banks, Dr. Phil, Montel Williams, and even Oprah Winfrey! I was totally unaware of it, and Mom and Dad were shooting all of them down so as not to interrupt my regular life. I was only six, and they weren't comfort-able with continuing to put me in the spotlight like that. They did ultimately agree to consider one offer, from *60 Minutes* in Australia, when I was in second grade, because it gave us an opportunity to educate an entire continent without affecting our privacy at home. After Mom and Dad discussed it with me and got the go-ahead, we shot a special that Dad stipulated could only air in Australia, to limit my media exposure in my everyday life.

I had a better grasp of what was at stake during that second big interview. Mom had been showing me all the positive messages she'd been getting through the TransKids Purple Rainbow Foundation website after *20/20* aired, as well as actual letters that the network forwarded to us. I couldn't believe how many people were affected by my story. The ones that hit me the hardest came from people who had been suicidal or had been physically attacked for being transgender.

One came in from a male-to-female transgender teen who had been about to leap off a building after her mom and dad told her they would rather have a dead son than a living transgender daughter. It's beyond me how parents could ever say something so brutal to their own child. The young woman wrote that as she was about to step off the roof she remembered one of my videos, and it gave her the courage to back away from the ledge.

Another message we received was from a very young transgender teenager who'd been stabbed and beaten so badly that she fell into a coma. When she finally recovered, she wrote and said the first time she smiled after the horrific incident was when someone showed her a video of me living a normal, happy life. She was inspired for the first time to become an advocate for transgender rights.

Dr. Marilyn knew how much these kinds of letters meant to me. Since she saw that I was comfortable talking about myself, she asked if Mom and I would be willing to speak to a class of first-year medical students at a nearby college. She was often asked by professors to speak at schools throughout Florida about transgender issues, and before long we were going with her every couple of months. Some classes were more intimate, and others took place in big auditoriums, which were a little more nerve-racking. Sometimes there would be other transgender patients of hers talking with us on a panel, but I was always the only kid. A student would ask a question and I'd sweat while trying to figure out what to say once it was my turn. But I quickly found that live public speaking came easily to me, even when I got asked ridiculous questions like whether I'd had complete gender reassignment surgery yet. I was eight! As crazy as the question seemed to me, though, it was an honest one. The student simply didn't know what sorts of options are available for gender reassignment (I'll get more into those later), and I realized it was pretty cool to have the chance to educate people.

The first really big panel I spoke on was at something called TransCon, an all-day conference in Miami devoted to transgender issues. There were a lot of familiar faces up on the stage with me—they were the same people I'd spoken with at the colleges, along with a woman I'd never met before named Rajee. I felt shy but I couldn't stop staring at her face—it was obvious that something had happened to it.

I soon learned that Rajee hadn't come out as transgender until she was in her twenties, after going through male puberty. Because she couldn't afford any sort of gender reassignment surgery, she went to a transgender woman in her neighborhood who promised she could give Rajee inexpensive fillers to help round out her face and hips, giving her a more womanly look. What Rajee didn't know was that not only was this woman unlicensed to do any sort of medical procedures, but she injected Rajee's body full of caulking cement, leaving her permanently disfigured. Rajee even woke up one morning with green pus oozing from her face. The "doctor" who did this to her ended up in jail and was charged with manslaughter after another one of her patients died.

It was yet another reminder of how lucky I was to have the family I do. I knew that because of their support I'd never have to go through what Rajee experienced. I gave her a huge hug after the panel. She told me how special and brave she thought I was, when in fact she was the brave one to have gone through what she did and still be so positive and willing to share her story. She's an inspiring role model.

Meeting Rajee really got me thinking about how being transgender affected the way I related to the world. There was something different about me, sure, but I didn't feel like it defined me as a person. I thought that sports and my love of art and acting and singing were the things that made me unique. When the 60 Minutes Australia reporter had asked me earlier in the year how I felt about having a girl brain and a boy body, I'd told her I felt fine.

"It's okay," I said. "It's like a normal life to me, pretty much, 'cause if people are making fun of you, just walk away and be friends with people that are nice to you and appreciate you."

That was exactly how I lived my life. And I was lucky to have a friend like Rebecca, who was especially nice to me. We continued having sleepovers and grew even closer in second grade. We were so crazy about each other that we decided we were going to get married. This didn't bother our parents. Rebecca's mom told us, "I don't care if she marries a boy or a girl as long as the person is Jewish!" For Valentine's Day that year, Rebecca and I even bought each other chocolates and teddy bears.

We constantly cracked each other up. We'd make crazy faces and repeat the same dumb jokes that we thought were hilarious, but there was one big problem with all that laughing. Since I wasn't allowed to use the regular bathrooms at school, I was holding it in a lot when I had to go. And when Rebecca made me laugh too hard, I'd pee my pants.

I started to come home with wet clothes, and sometimes the accident would be bad enough that the school had to call my mom to bring me a whole new outfit. Instead of being embarrassed when kids would laugh at me, I was more like, *Screw it.* It wasn't my fault I was in that situation! I blamed the school for leaving me with such terrible choices: the in-classroom bathroom with absolutely no privacy, the long, humiliating trek to the nurse's bathroom, or having accidents. Mom felt really bad for me. She understood why it kept happening and made a point of reminding Ms. Reynolds whenever she dropped off clean clothes.

After a while I started to get really fed up. Our school had an open-air plan, with a big circular courtyard in the center and outdoor pathways that led to the different buildings, sort of like an octopus shape. You could see into all the buildings when you were outside, including the doors that led to the bathrooms. I started to keep my eye on the nearest girls' room doors and count how many people were going in and out. Whenever I was sure one was empty, I'd run inside, lock myself in a stall and pee, and then clear out as fast as I could.

One day I was sitting in the library, which had a big window in its door that looked right out onto the bathroom on the other side of the hallway. I had to pee so badly that I had my legs crossed. I thumped my ankle against my calf while I waited and counted, and as soon as I was sure the coast was clear I jumped up and ran out of the library. As I was opening the bathroom door, I happened to glance over my shoulder, just in time to see the school librarian staring at me with a scarily stern look on her face.

It was too late, though. My body knew how close I was to relief and so I shut the door and did what I'd gone there to do. When I came out, the librarian was standing in the hallway waiting for me with her arms crossed.

"You know you're not allowed in there," she said.

"I really had to go," I said, looking at my feet.

"There are specific bathrooms for you. You know that."

"I know," I mumbled. "But . . ."

"The principal needs to know about this," she said. She went back into the library and left me in the hall.

I spent the rest of the day in dread, waiting to get pulled out of class. But it never happened. The librarian must have had a change of heart.

I stopped trying to sneak into the girls' bathroom after that and went back to peeing my pants. The following year, we finally got the school to stop forcing me to wear skorts by securing a waiver to opt out of the dress code. (We hadn't realized this was something students were allowed to do, but it could only happen during the first ten days of school. The first year we didn't know about the policy, and the second year we found out after the deadline and they wouldn't make an exception for me.)

One day, I had on a pair of thin shorts and underwear when I peed myself. The undies managed to catch most of the mess, so I slunk to the nurse's bathroom, undressed, wadded them up in a bunch of toilet paper, and buried them in the trash can. It wasn't until I walked back out into the hallway that I glanced down and realized that without underwear to tuck it away, the outline of my penis was now visible through the fabric. I shuffled down the hallway hunched over a little, trying to maneuver my body in a way that would make my penis move farther back between my legs. That didn't work, so I folded my hands, very ladylike, and kept them in front of me. I spent the time until my shorts finally dried walking around with either a book or a piece of paper held below my waist, blocking the view. I tried to laugh it off in my head to keep away the creeping sense of shame I felt, but even as self-confident as I was, it didn't really work.

The whole situation was like a real-life version of that dream people have where they're standing in front of the classroom and suddenly realize they're naked. But it was worse because I felt doubly exposed—it wasn't just that my genitals were showing. They were the wrong kind.

My success at soccer helped give me the confidence to get through some tough social situations in school and still feel good about myself.

CHAPTER 7

"I'm only friends with people who will accept me for who I am no matter what, and not for what's between my legs."

I'm the first to admit it—when I hit third grade, I started getting a little full of myself. I was kicking butt in travel soccer but had no clue about the struggle my parents were going through to secure a legitimate place for me on the team. I was getting straight As and made the honor roll, and still got picked first in gym class all the time. I was beating Rebecca in sports, and even though she was a great student, she wasn't doing as well as me academically, and I found myself feeling competitive with her.

One day she called me out on it. She told me I was selfish and bratty, and I told her she was rude, and after that our engagement was off. We weren't going to get married after all. More immediately, it meant I needed a new best friend.

There was another girl in my grade who I was pretty friendly with named Casey. She was a tall girl and incredibly pretty, with long straight blond hair. I marched up to her during lunch, looked way up so I could make eye contact, and said, "Hey, do you want to be my new best friend?"

She said sure, and that was that.

It was weird to suddenly have a new best friend who I didn't really know at all, but we went with it, and I'm so happy we did because she is still my best friend to this day.

Rebecca and I didn't become enemies or anything. Our big fight just sort of faded away, like they do when you're a kid. We were still buddies, but we had outgrown each other. She and Casey and I all sat together during lunch, though, along with a trio of girls named Megan, Jessica, and Brittney.

These three girls were hard for me to understand. My lunch period didn't always overlap with Casey's and Rebecca's, so some days I'd eat with the trio alone. For a week they would be super nice and friendly to me, and then out of nowhere I'd sit down next to them and they'd scoot away and ignore me. I'd get up and find someone else to sit with, totally confused about what had just happened. But then the next day Rebecca and Casey would be back and everything would be fine, and I'd wonder if it had all been in my head because they never said anything mean to my face. And when they'd start being nice to me again, they were *really* nice.

I had a lot going on to distract me from their odd behavior. In addition to soccer, I played flag football that year and was good enough to make the all-star team! I was one of only two girls, although the game announcer forgot that one night when we were all heading out onto the field. It was standard for him to introduce each player over the loudspeaker and tell the crowd a little bit about his or her game history, and when I walked out all I could hear was "Jaron, blah blah HE blah blah then HE blah blah . . ."

I was mortified, and I could hear confused murmurs from the stands. I didn't know it at the time, but my dad, who happened to know a guy who was in the booth with the announcer, was furiously texting him from the bleachers, telling him to let the announcer know he needed to correct his mistake. Sure enough, as soon as I made a good play I heard over the loudspeakers: "An amazing move from Jaron, SHE maneuvered HER way right around blah blah . . ."

It felt good to hear people correct mistakes like that, but toward the end of the year, the trio of girls I ate lunch with started acting ruder and ruder to me, and then on the very last day of school I heard a rumor that they no longer wanted to sit with "the transgender girl." I finally asked Casey what the deal with them was.

"Oh, they hate you," she said.

"What?!"

"Yeah, they think you're selfish and don't like you at all."

Casey wasn't telling me that to be mean. She's always

had my back and is just brutally honest, not the type to sugarcoat anything. That being said, I don't think she thought I'd take it so hard, since I acted so confident. I had always made a big deal about how if people didn't like me, I didn't need them in my life. I'd go out and find people who were kind and liked me for who I was. But this was different. These girls had pretended to be my friends for months but were talking behind my back the whole time.

I went home crying that day. Up until then, it had always been easy to tell if a person didn't like me. They either told me to my face, or put out a nasty vibe that was easy to pick up on. What those girls had done felt like a sneak attack. I know backstabbing happens all the time, especially in school, but it was new to me then and it hurt badly.

This experience really shook my confidence. I stopped talking to everyone from school that summer and instead focused on Next Stop Broadway. I had continued going every year since I'd started but still hadn't gotten a big role.

The previous year I'd done all three sessions. During the first one I got to get up onstage and hula-hoop for the audience before the performance of *Alice in Wonderland*. In the second session we did *Seussical* and I got my first and only lead as the somewhat snarky Young Kangaroo, daughter of the Sour Kangaroo. (To be truthful, it was a pretty small part, but still considered a lead!) Third session was *The Little Mermaid*, and it really sucked when I didn't get any kind of major role for that one, for obvious reasons.

I made some close friends at the camp, including a girl

named Erin. The two of us would always team up for Spirit Rally—a chance for the kids to perform anything they wanted in front of the others. Erin and I came up with a whole choreographed routine to that Cascada song, "Everytime We Touch." I hoped it would catch the teachers' attention and show them I was worthy of a starring part, but it didn't work. I kept up my determination, though, because I wanted to act. Anytime an audition approached I'd rehearse and rehearse and rehearse, and then still not get a part. I'd give my all to whatever small role they tossed my way—I was a good sport like that—but I couldn't figure out why I wasn't getting cast. I'd videotape myself practicing songs and play the recording back to pick out spots I needed to work on. I was a perfectionist, and I knew I was just as good as (if not better than!) any of the kids who were getting chosen.

My confidence started to waver, though, as I continued to get passed over for roles. I had a deeper voice than the other girls, and I started to wonder if that was the problem. My mom had a theory that made more sense. Since girls outnumbered boys at the camp by around ten to one, a lot of times the director would have to cast a girl in a boy's part. Everyone there knew I was transgender, and since theater people tend to be pretty liberal, it was no big deal. Except that there was a chance I wasn't getting parts because the director was worried about offending me by casting me as a male. I would have been fine with it! Theater is about pretending to be someone you *aren't*, not who you actually are!

I was nervous about returning to school for fourth grade. I hadn't spoken to Casey at all over the summer, and for some reason I genuinely thought she wouldn't remember who I was. I saw her from across the room right before the first-day orientation started, and she was wearing a bright orange shirt. I'd started to approach her shyly when she screamed out my name, rushed through the crowd, and grabbed me up in a huge hug.

I guess she really is still my best friend, I thought.

We caught each other up on what we'd done over the summer break before going to our separate classes. When I got back to mine, I saw a girl named Olivia, who I'd talked to a few times the year before, walk into the room. I was still wrapped up in the excitement of the first day and my joy at how happy Casey was to see me, so I reached out and gave Olivia a hug as she walked by.

"It's so good to see you!" I said.

"Ew," she said, and quickly pulled her backpack off her shoulders and started dramatically wiping her entire body off with it. "You got your cooties *all* over me!"

I tried to not let it bother me, but it sort of ended up ruining the first couple of days of school. I couldn't understand why she was so rude! I bounced back pretty fast, though, and decided to focus on how cool it was to be at school with Casey again. I hoped we'd end up in the same classes that year, but sadly we were assigned different classes.

My busy soccer schedule meant I didn't get to see Casey

much at all that year. I ended up becoming friends with a girl in my gifted class named Lisa, who was a Jehovah's Witness. I was sort of fascinated with her religion—she didn't celebrate her birthday or any holidays. It seemed a little strange to me, but I accepted it as part of who she was.

By that age I was telling anyone who became a friend that I was transgender. I was old enough that my mom no longer did it for me when it came to my friends' parents, but our disclosure rule was still in full effect. I wasn't allowed to go to anyone's house unless everyone knew I was trans and was cool with it.

I don't know how many people in the school actually knew about me at that point aside from the teachers, because the ones I told were friends like Casey who weren't the type to gossip. The three mean girls from the previous year's lunch were still around, but as far as I knew they weren't spreading any more rumors about me.

I understood that Lisa might be a little trickier to come out to because she had such a strict religious background. We kept talking about having a sleepover, so I knew I couldn't put it off much longer. I ended up showing her the Barbara Walters video and the one we'd shot for *60 Minutes* Australia, hoping it would answer all her questions and make her realize that there were other people in the world like me.

She was totally accepting, and I explained the rule that she had to tell her parents about me before I could spend the night at her house.

The next day I noticed right away that Lisa had a hard time looking me in the eyes, and within a couple of days we were barely talking at all. It was obvious that her parents and their religious beliefs were not accepting of me.

I understood the situation and moved on with my head held high. But it wasn't long before a girl I didn't even know came up to me in music class and said, "Alicia is telling everyone you're a chick with a dick."

I froze. *Who the heck is Alicia?* "Wow, really?" I asked.

"Is it true?"

I turned around and left the girl standing there. As I walked away I searched around in my heart to try to figure out how I felt. I was a little shocked by how nasty the language was, but other than that, I felt strangely light. That was when it hit me—I *genuinely* didn't care what other people thought about me.

It was such a freeing sensation. This was around the same time that I had gone back to practicing with my old travel soccer team but wasn't allowed to play actual games, and I started comparing the two types of bigotry happening in my life.

The prejudice I was experiencing with the state soccer association had big implications. I knew that battle had the power to create change, and that was where I should focus my energy. But playground insults? I wasn't about to let those touch me when I had larger things to face. Not that I had any intention of letting this Alicia girl get away with saying such a mean thing—I immediately told the principal what she was saying—but I knew it was pointless to get upset about her when there were more important things at stake.

Alicia's big mouth actually ended up sparking some pretty helpful conversations. Some of the braver girls in my class came up to me on the playground and asked if it was true what she had been saying. I told them, "Yes, I'm transgender." They'd ask me all sorts of questions and I'd answer them. Even though a lot of the kids were the tougher ones in our school, they were basically just curious and were totally fine with me after I talked to them and explained my situation in a calm, normal way.

I had recently gotten into writing and became inspired to create a song that I still sing to myself when I'm feeling down:

I am myself
And I would fly through the sky
Swim through the sea
To be whoever I want to be
Because I am myself
And I want to be free!

The song is punctuated by a lot of "yeahs," and I draw out the word "myself" so it's more like "maaaah-seeellllfff." What can I say, singing makes me happy!

I found out much later that after I talked to the principal about Alicia, she called her mother to tell her what had happened, and she was horrified that her daughter would use that kind of language about another person, and especially someone who was LGBT. Turns out Alicia's mom's brother was gay, and she'd thought she had raised her daughter to be an open and accepting person. And I bet you anything that after that day, she was. The whole experience helped me understand I had been wrong about shrugging off name-calling—the little fights can be just as important as the big ones.

I always enjoy my days at the Philadelphia
Trans-Health Conference, working for the cause.
Helping others is so important to me.

CHAPTER 8

"I want boobs."

My life kind of exploded when I started fifth grade. So much crazy stuff happened! To begin with, we started going to the Philadelphia Trans-Health Conference again. We'd had to skip the previous few years because of scheduling conflicts, but we returned the summer before fifth grade started and decided to host our own workshop on transitioning while you're young. In addition to ours, I attended a panel about teenagers who have transitioned, and I introduced the two speakers. They shared their stories and showed photographs of themselves before and after their transitions, and when they opened up the panel to questions from the audience, the two teens invited me back up onstage with them to participate. Someone asked:

If we were handed a magic wand and told we could suddenly not be transgender, and instead be placed directly into the body we desired, would we do it? The first guy on the panel, whose name was Adam, said yes, because he was a singer and had made the decision not to take testosterone because it would likely deepen his voice. The second person on the panel also said yes, because she wanted to have a baby someday but wouldn't be able to because she wasn't born with a uterus.

I'd love to have a baby of my own someday, too, and the audience member's question made me think of that old dream I'd had with the Good Fairy and her magic wand. But my life had changed so much since then, and all for the better. Before I knew what was happening, I started to tear up right there in front of the whole roomful of people. "I'd break the wand in half," I said. "I'm proud of who I am."

I didn't mean it as a slight to the other two panelists; I just realized in that moment that being transgender had made me the person I'd become. And I really liked that person.

The workshop my family hosted later, on transitioning as a kid, was such a success that we decided to offer it every year. Since the people who show up tend to get really emotional (including us), we now jokingly call it the Love Fest in the workshop description, and the nickname quickly caught on with everyone.

It had been a couple of years since we'd done any sort of media stuff, so when Oprah's OWN network contacted us about doing a mini-documentary with them, we were wary at first. We were busy just living our lives: Mom was really involved with TransKids Purple Rainbow Foundation, the twins were total rock stars on their football and soccer teams, Ari was singing in a band, and we all went to each other's events and supported each other. But my dad got deeper and deeper into the soccer battle, and I felt myself growing more and more comfortable talking about transgender issues around school and not just at panel discussions, so we eventually agreed as a family to participate in the OWN show.

It was a way bigger production than either of the TV interviews we'd done before. For one thing, it lasted two weeks, and the camera people would do things like come into our house before the sun even rose to watch us wake up. That was definitely a little weird—no one looks good when they roll out of bed, and it was hard to think of anything interesting to say to the camera in my face when all I wanted to do was shower and brush my teeth!

While we were shooting, I went for my annual physical and got some news that freaked me out—I had already started puberty. I hadn't been expecting that at all. The twins didn't start puberty until they were thirteen! When they had their bar mitzvahs, there was nothing going on, but then suddenly, BAM. They shot up a few inches, grew facial hair, got acne, and started smelling like teenage boys.

But I had only just turned eleven, so puberty wasn't on our minds at all yet. My parents and I had already researched options for me in terms of taking hormone blockers to suppress my body's male development when the time came, but we had figured that was a year away at the very least. At my physical, the doctor poked around between my legs and announced that I'd already entered something called Tanner 2. The Tanner scale is a method of tracking puberty development, and for male bodies, stage 2 meant that my testes were beginning to grow bigger.

I didn't panic. I understood that we'd caught it early and that we still had time before anything drastic happened. The most that might occur between then and the time it took for me to get my blockers was that I might grow a couple of pubic hairs.

They were already starting to sprout up, but in numbers I could count on one hand.

For the puberty blockers, I had two options. There was Lupron, which is a suppressor that you inject into your butt every month, or Supprelin, a tiny implant that gets embedded in your arm and releases medicine over time, anywhere from one to three years. That was the option I wanted. I'm not afraid of needles at all; it's just that I was more into the idea of only having to deal with the treatment every couple of years, when the implant gets swapped out for a new one. Even though I'd have to get knocked out each time they replaced one, it felt like the easier option.

The idea with blockers is that they would give me time to figure out what I wanted to do about my male body later in life, without developing things like facial hair, a lower voice, an Adam's apple, and other male characteristics. For a long time when I was younger I'd had the same nightmare over and over about giant beards and mustaches chasing me and trying to attach themselves to my face.

With the blockers, I'd be able to pick the time that was right for me to start taking estrogen to help me develop into a more feminine body, and then possibly have surgery somewhere down the line. I knew I was still too young to make those kinds of decisions.

It's really important to understand that not every transgender person decides to go this route, and many aren't fortunate enough to even *have* blockers as an option. They don't have the family, medical, or financial support that I did. I really want to stress that every single person's transition is different. Some people choose surgery and hormones, and some don't. It's a deeply personal process, and as a rule you should never ask a person who is transgender about what options they've taken—if any—unless they offer to start up that conversation themselves.

I get that there's a natural curiosity for a lot of people who are unfamiliar with transgender surgery options, but if you're really interested, take the initiative to educate yourself through the Internet. All the information is out there to discover on your own, without putting a transgender person on the spot. I've included some great informational websites in the Resources section at the end of this book.

Anyway, taking the blockers was what I knew was right for me at that time, and not a day goes by when I don't appreciate how incredibly lucky I am to have parents who allowed me to choose this option.

Making this decision was only the beginning of the process. There ended up being a couple of problems before I was able to start taking the blockers. The first was that my doctor couldn't find a surgeon who was willing to place the implant in my arm, so we had to find a new doctor who had an associate who would agree to do it. Mildly annoying, but I tried to not let it bother me. The next problem was that we had to order the implant and the applicator (a handheld device that sort of looks like a medical-grade Mini Be Dazzler) by mail. Since our insurance wouldn't cover either, my parents shopped around until they found a less expensive version of the medication. Mom ordered it through a company in Canada, and they in turn ordered it from a company in the UK. The medicine had to travel from the UK to us via FedEx, but on its way across the American border, the border patrol confiscated it. So we had to wait several more weeks while the company shipped a replacement to us via regular mail.

When we finally arrived for the procedure, the doctor asked Mom to hand everything over and she happily gave him the applicator.

"Where's the implant?" he asked, referring to the teeny tiny cylinder that shoots out of the applicator's nozzle.

I watched her face change from confusion to horror. She thought the implant was already inside the device, but

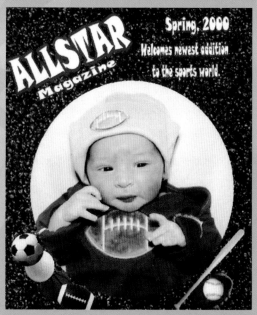

With the third boy and fourth child, our family was complete—or so we thought. . . .

Stilettos at fifteen months!

Our family, the way we were, with Princess Ari at the center.

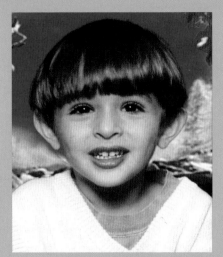

A boy's bowl cut at age three. Humiliating!

The moment at my preschool dance recital when my mother recognized my distress at not being able to dress and dance like the girls. Notice the look of hurt and confusion on my face.

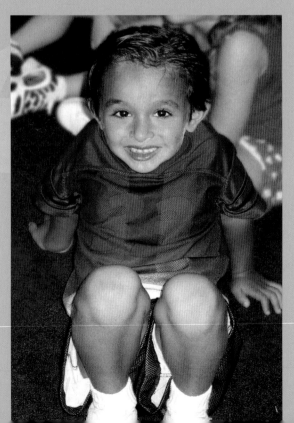

Mom's last attempt to dress me as a boy for school.

At home, I was all girl!

My inner princess would
not stay hidden.

Everyone's first day of school—and my last first day of preschool. Notice
that I still had to wear boy shorts, but I could wear my princess shirt proudly.

My fifth birthday . . . my coming-out day.

My first outing presenting as a girl, at Disney, with the right pronoun.

Finally, by the end of preschool, I was allowed to wear the Ema (Mommy) apron at our Sabbath celebration. Notice the pearls on the apron—they meant everything to me!

This is me in Pre-K when I had to dress like a boy. 😊

This is me in Kindergarten. I look like a girl now! 😊

Art has always helped me express my feelings.

I was letting my hair grow in and calling myself Sparkles—see my T-shirt.

I loved cheerleading when I was little.

I wasn't getting big roles at Next Stop Broadway, so I created roles for myself at home—like this beautiful zombie.

Aspiring mermaid on the half shell!

Banned from girls' travel soccer.

Having to sit on the bench and not being able to help my team was one of my most painful experiences.

It was great to be back on the field again after the ban was lifted.

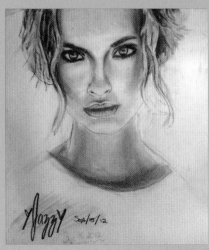

Drawing was one of the ways I dealt with my disappointment and depression. By the time I was eleven, my technique had greatly improved.

If my dad hadn't fought a two-and-a-half-year legal battle for my right to play soccer, I wouldn't be back on the field doing something I love.

I was thrilled to appear on *The Rosie Show* with Chaz Bono, who grew up on TV as Cher and Sonny Bono's famous daughter and transitioned to male as an adult. (left to right) Chaz, me, Mom, and Rosie.

it turned out that it had been packaged separately in the box. My mom had thrown it out!

Thankfully the doctor had been treating a child with precocious puberty, which is when a kid enters puberty at a *really* young age, so he had some extra Lupron lying around. After all that, I ended up having to get the butt shot anyway. I could feel the liquid course through me as soon as the needle went in, but other than that I didn't feel any different physically.

Since it took so long for our replacement implant to arrive, I ended up having to get the shot three more times over the next several months. Four butt shots later, I was finally ready to get that little sucker implanted under my skin.

For the initial injection the doctor only used a local anesthetic, so I was awake for the whole thing. He invited my new physician, Dr. Charlton, to watch him so he'd be able to inject me himself when it was time to do it again. I didn't watch what was going on, but I could hear the step-by-step explanation of everything that was happening. The implant stays on the underside of my upper left arm, and basically all they did was cut me open, stick the nozzle inside, and pop the cylinder out inside me.

Mom recorded the whole thing, and it's pretty gross to watch. I had no idea my skin was so elastic—it looks like they were stretching a pair of pantyhose up off my arm when they created the little tunnel for the implant to go into.

The doctor stitched me up, and that was that. The reason I have to be put to sleep to swap out the implant with a new one when the medicine runs out is because after the implant has been inside my body for so long, the muscle and tissue grow around it and it needs to be surgically cut out. I don't like touching the implant because it rises above my skin a little bit so I can feel the ridges, and it weirds me out. But it's better than having an Adam's apple sticking out of my neck.

Not long after I got the implant, I began to notice that the girls at school were starting puberty. (Even though we were all the same age, they were right on time, since girl bodies usually begin puberty a year or two earlier than boy bodies. I shouldn't have started puberty for another year or two.) The differences were small at first, things like acne popping up on their faces, which I was definitely not jealous about. Once they began to develop breasts, I understandably got self-conscious. My doctor thought it was still too early for me to go on estrogen and begin growing boobs myself, so I started to wear Ari's hand-me-down bras to school. For over a year I'd been keeping them in a drawer marked SOMETHING FOR THE FUTURE. OR NOW. Even though my chest was flat, there was enough padding in the bra to make it look like there was at least *something* happening there under my shirt.

I'd tried a similar tactic the year before, but Mom wouldn't let me leave the house. One morning I had put on one of Ari's old bras, wadded up some socks, and stuck them inside the cups. I maneuvered them around until they looked even and walked downstairs to the kitchen as if nothing were different.

"What is that?" Mom yelled as she looked up from the table. "Uh-uh, no way. You're not fooling anyone."

"What are you talking about?" I asked, trying to sound as innocent as possible.

"Jaron, get upstairs and take that off right now. No one is going to believe that you magically sprouted boobs overnight."

"But don't they look real?" I asked, trying not to get too upset.

"Okay, to be fair, you did a good job getting them to look symmetrical, but they're way too big. And it's dishonest. We are not a dishonest family."

"Fine," I grumbled, and marched back up to my room. I wasn't as angry as I pretended to be. The socks were getting itchy against my skin, and the idea of trying to keep up the scam and make them look exactly the same every day was already starting to seem exhausting.

Once I was allowed to wear the padded bras, I wondered if I would start to get noticed by boys at school. But it turned out to be the OWN documentary that landed me my first boyfriend.

Dressed for a TV appearance to promote the OWN
documentary that won me my first "boyfriend."

CHAPTER 9

"Everyone deserves to be loved."

In elementary school, it's normal to get a friend to ask someone out for you. What's not so normal is when a guy convinces his mother to call the girl's mom and have *her* ask her daughter out on a date for him. I'd say that's a pretty solid warning sign that the relationship is doomed from the start.

I definitely thought it was unusual when Zack's mom first approached mine, but (a) I was starting to get curious about what dating would be like for me, since I'd never had a boyfriend, and (b) it turned out that Zack was really cute.

Even though none of my friends were interested in boys yet, I knew based on what I'd seen Ari go through that guys were probably going to start becoming a thing in our lives before too long. I don't think she was ever without a boyfriend, and if someone was offering me the chance to get a head start, I figured I'd better take it.

Mom was at one of Griffen and Sander's soccer matches when she got a call from Dad's secretary. A woman had been calling the office all morning begging to be put in touch with her. This person said she needed to discuss her son, which was why my mother agreed to call her back. She assumed this parent needed help with her transgender kid, although it was a little odd that a stranger had managed to track down where Dad worked instead of reaching out through Facebook or the TransKids Purple Rainbow Foundation site.

It turned out that the only help this woman needed was with micromanaging her child's dating life. (Kidding, kidding. She was actually very sweet.) Her son Zack had been watching television with his mom one day when they flipped past a daytime talk show I had been on earlier in the year to promote the OWN documentary. Zack's mother explained to my mom that he had immediately started jumping up and down and telling her, "That's the girl I'm in love with!" She probably wouldn't have thought anything more about it except that he started to lose sleep and talk about me constantly. His mom was worried about how strong his reaction was, and so she reached out to us to see if I'd be willing to talk to him.

I normally wouldn't have agreed to meet with a total

stranger who had a crush on me, except it turned out that I vaguely knew who Zack was. He went to my school, but he was a year younger than me. Apparently he'd been watching me in the hallways, too scared to come up and say hello. I even remembered that at one point he'd passed by me and blurted, "I saw you on TV!" before running away. I hadn't thought anything of it at the time, since by then I was used to random people casually mentioning that they'd seen me on TV, but after I learned that Zack liked me, I started to look at him in a whole new way. He had long wavy blond hair and beautiful blue eyes. Plus his smile was enormous—it lit up his whole face like a sunbeam whenever he grinned.

After clearing it with me, my mom told his mom that he could reach out to me on Facebook. His first message was "Hi, can I be your boyfriend?"

In my mind I was all, *Slow down, dude!* I wanted to be polite, so I explained that no, he couldn't be my boyfriend because I didn't even know him, but we could be friends and talk.

That status didn't last long, though. We quickly became a Facebook couple, which meant that even though we initially didn't see a lot of each other outside school since we were in different grades, our messages usually went something like this:

ZACK: UR hot

ME: UR hotter!

ZACK: *When we get married it's gonna be the best!*

ME: *I wonder what our grandkids will look like.*

I understand now that we were just mimicking what we *thought* a relationship should look like, and we wrote the things we believed a boyfriend and girlfriend were supposed to say to each other. It was like the preteen version of playing house.

For our first official date, we decided to go to a carnival that had arrived in town. I put a lot of thought into what to wear that night, even though I'd stopped caring so much about fashion after I grew out of my sparkly/rainbow/princess phase when I was around seven. I wanted to look my best without overdressing and decided to go casual cute with a pair of jeans (instead of the usual cutoffs that I made myself) and a green sweater.

Our dads came with us as chaperones, but we were allowed to run off on our own, and we held hands under the flashing colored lights of the midway. We got a rush from the smell of popcorn and cotton candy mixed with grease from the rickety rides. They looked like they were about three seconds away from busting a cable and flinging people off into the night sky, but we rode all of them anyway.

Our next date, to a science museum, wasn't as adventurous, but it was still fun running around, holding hands, and playing with all the interactive exhibits.

By our third date, I was determined to get my first kiss. Zack really wanted to go see *The Hunger Games*, and even though I'd already seen it I said I hadn't, just to hurry things along. I didn't have time to debate which movie to watch—I just wanted that kiss!

Despite planning our future family when we wrote to each other online, in person Zack could still be shy. So I knew it was going to be up to me to make the first move, and I had a genius plan in place.

Since I'd already watched the movie, I knew how heart-breaking Rue's death scene is. When it happened this time around in the theater with Zack, I pretended to be shocked and sad and in need of comfort. I turned to him, grabbed his face, and kissed him. There was no tongue, but we held our lips together for a pretty long time.

He pulled away first, and I could see him sitting there with a huge grin on his face. I replayed the moment in my mind and decided it had been a good first kiss, but I knew I wanted to try more. I kept sneaking glances over at him to see if there'd be another opportunity, when suddenly he told me he had a really bad stomachache. I watched as he stood up and shuffled out of the row and walked down the aisle to where his mom, our chaperone for the date, was sitting. I was mortified. He wasn't acting like he felt sick, and I became convinced that I had bad breath. *What if his supposed stomachache is just an excuse to get away from me?* I thought.

I watched him huddle with his mom for a few minutes before he made his way back up to me.

"Are you okay?" I asked, worried. They'd been whispering for an awfully long time considering we were all in the middle of watching a movie. Then it dawned on me.

"Wait, did you just go and tell your mother that we kissed?" I asked.

"Yeah," he admitted.

Great, I thought. The ride home, with his mom grinning at me from the rearview mirror every two seconds, could not have ended fast enough.

That night, I told my brothers what had happened and they yelled at me, saying girls are never supposed to make the first move. I wasn't about to stand for that crap, though. When I know what I want, I'm going to go after it.

"Maybe I just have bigger balls than him," I snapped. They cracked up, but I regretted my choice of words immediately. Seeing how Zack was a year younger than me, it was probably literally true, and this was the last thing about myself that I wanted to be reminded of.

A big part of my time with Zack was discovering what I was and wasn't cool with in terms of the gender roles that come along with relationships. When he would try to hold doors open for me, I'd get really defiant. Who decided that as a girl I couldn't open a stupid door for myself? A part of me got that he was only being polite, but that came from an idea that women are weak, and I hated that. Whenever he would open a door for me at school I'd insist that he close it and let me open it back up for myself.

Feeling that assertiveness, along with the safety of knowing that male puberty wasn't going to hit because of my new hormone blockers, really helped build up my dating confidence. But on our next movie night, disaster struck.

I don't remember exactly what I ate that day that caused my intestinal distress, but when he and his mom came to pick me up, I opened the car door, flopped down on the backseat, and accidentally ripped one.

I froze, waiting to see if Zack or his mom would say anything, and prayed that they just thought it was the sound of me hitting the seat. But I couldn't leave it alone and asked Zack, "Did you hear that?"

"No, no, I didn't hear anything," he answered, a little too quickly.

Screw it, I thought. *These things happen. We're all human.* I just thanked God it hadn't smelled.

But my butt wasn't done with me yet.

The movie we were seeing was the Disney film *Chimpanzee*. I guess I can take some comfort in the fact that we were watching a nature film, since what happened next is just part of nature, after all.

I accidentally did it again, loudly and distinctly smelly.

I couldn't even look at Zack. Even though he was sitting right next to me, I pulled out my phone and texted him.

ME: *I'm so embarrassed right now.*

ZACK: *Why?*

ME: *Because I just farted really loud and it smells bad and I feel awful.*

ZACK: *I couldn't even tell. It's fine. Don't worry about it.*

That kid was a saint for lying, but I still couldn't face him. I did, however, figure I should take advantage of his nobleness.

ME: *Do you want to kiss now so I can feel better?*

ZACK: *Sure.*

Fifth-grade crushes are so weird.

On that day we kissed even longer, but we still kept our mouths closed. It was nearing the end of the school year, and I was determined to *really* make out with him before I started middle school. I knew I had the whole summer to make it happen, but the last day of school presented a perfect opportunity—Griffen and Sander were throwing an end-of-the-year party at our house. There would be tons of teenagers running all over the place, creating the perfect distraction for my parents if I could just get Zack alone somewhere.

Once the party was raging, I snuck Zack up to my room

and shut the door. We got on the bed and cuddled together for a few minutes before I climbed on top of him.

Here goes, I thought. I closed my eyes, leaned down, and kissed him. I opened my mouth, but the second my tongue touched Zack's lips he pushed my face away.

"Ouch, you just bit me!" he said, covering his mouth with his hand.

At the exact same moment, my dad walked into the room. His eyes popped out like a cartoon character's.

"What is going on here?" he demanded.

I leapt off the bed and insisted we were just hanging out. I could tell that Dad didn't believe it for a second, and he told us to get downstairs and join the party. When we reached the backyard, Zack wandered over to the food table, still rubbing his lip. Sander happened to be walking by so I grabbed his arm, dragged him into the playroom, and shut the door.

I began to explain what had just happened, but I suddenly started crying. Everything had gone downhill so fast, and I was only just then absorbing the reality of the situation.

"Wait, so did you actually bite him?" Sander asked.

"No!" I wailed. "Of course not. But what if my tongue is razor sharp and I never knew it?"

"Don't be ridiculous," Sander said. "He probably just freaked out and that was the only thing he could think of to say. Don't worry about it, and try again later. Think of it this way—you'd have cut up your own mouth years ago if your tongue was that dangerous."

He gave me a hug and got me to stop crying. My brothers always know how to cheer me up. I thanked him and went back out to the party in search of my boyfriend.

Zack clearly wasn't interested in me anymore. He refused all my suggestions that we go somewhere to be alone, and he seemed nervous and distracted. Before too long his mom showed up to drive him home.

And that was that. We never spoke again. At one point around the middle of the summer, I texted him just to confirm that we had broken up, and he wrote back that we were no good for each other. He was right, of course. I was getting ready to start middle school, and the idea of having a boyfriend who was still in elementary school was too weird, even for someone like me who doesn't care about societal norms. I wasn't too sad about losing him in the end, but I was *very* bummed that I hadn't gotten to make out.

I get so excited about roller coasters that I wore this extremely large bow to make sure I was tall enough to get on the ride with my dad.

CHAPTER 10

"I should be able to use the bathroom. It's just a bathroom. You're making such a big deal about it."

Zack wasn't my only disastrous setup in fifth grade. My mom had an acquaintance with a daughter my age, and this woman was very pushy about getting us to hang out together. This girl, Sarah, was nice enough, but it felt really awkward to be set up on a playdate with someone I didn't know at all, and whose mom didn't even know my mom very well. It had been one thing to go through that with Zack because there had been a chance at romance, but I wasn't really looking for any new friends in my life. I didn't have anything in common with Sarah, but like I said, she was nice. So I didn't think twice when I accepted her invitation to visit a carnival that was going on a couple of hours away from where we lived.

I haven't mentioned this yet, but I am *obsessed* with roller coasters. Completely, utterly obsessed. Whenever my family plans a summer vacation, I always check out what route we're taking way beforehand and see if there are any theme parks with good rides along the way that we can stop at. The first roller coaster I ever went on was Manta at Sea World, on my tenth birthday a year earlier. It was a special trip that I took with just my dad, and I was so scared that I wouldn't be tall enough to ride the coaster that I wore a gigantic bow in my hair and ripped the insoles out of three different pairs of shoes to put inside the ones I was wearing to make me taller. Not that I recommend that any other kids do this, but it worked! (Also, it was only a matter of a one-inch difference; my dad never would have let me do anything unsafe!)

Since I knew there would be a roller coaster at the carnival Sarah invited me to, I figured I was guaranteed a good time. She and her dad came to pick me up in the afternoon and we slept the whole ride there. When we arrived I was groggy and out of it, so I decided there was no better way to wake myself up than to get right down to business. We jumped on the first coaster we came to, a medium-size ride designed to be taken apart so it could be easily moved to the carnival's next location. My safety belt was kind of loose, and as soon as we shot down the first big hill my head slammed against the side of the seat so hard I almost blacked out. The next thing I knew, the ride was over. I stumbled off, thinking I might have gotten a concussion. But I didn't want to say anything and ruin the trip for everyone else, so I kept my mouth shut and kept going on rides, even as the pain in my head grew worse and worse, until it blew into a full-on migraine. At least, that was what I figured it had to be. My head had never hurt that bad before, and I knew my mom got migraines. I powered on, though, determined to try to have fun, even though every time Sarah screamed on a ride I was convinced that a hundred tiny nails were being driven into my brain.

My body finally gave up on me when we got on the Pirate Ship, one of those big fake boats that swings back and forth, really high up in the air on each end. Once it got going and rocked all the way up to the point where my body was parallel to the ground, I looked down at all the people on the other side of the ship below me. I made eye contact with a girl and she smiled, and then her eyes got real big as I opened my mouth and vomit started to pour out of it.

"Oooooooh, we got a puker!" I heard her scream just as the ride dropped back down. I tried to aim off the side of the ship, but most of my lunch ended up on my face.

No one was screaming for fun anymore. They were all trying to dodge the spray coming from inside my stomach as the ship continued to hurtle back and forth. I did everything I could to keep it from hitting anyone, but you can't fight gravity and physics.

As soon as the ride stopped I ran as far away as I could, straight to a bathroom, where I did my best to clean myself up. Sarah followed me in and helped, saying nice things like "It's not that bad," even though we both knew it was. My breath reeked, my shirt was covered in stains, and no matter how many times I rinsed and brushed my hair out with my fingers, I kept finding more vomit hidden deeper and deeper within the strands.

When we'd finally managed to get me as clean as possible, we left the bathroom and found Sarah's dad waiting for us.

"You feeling any better?" he asked as Sarah looked on, still concerned.

Despite my appearance, smell, and headache, I did. At least I wasn't nauseous anymore, and was actually a little hungry, so I happily took him up on his offer to buy us ice cream to try to make it all better.

I ordered my favorite, a chocolate milk shake. As I lifted it up to my mouth to take that first delicious cool sip, the lid suddenly popped off and the entire shake slopped out all over the front of my shirt.

I didn't have any energy left to scream. I looked up at her dad and asked if we could go home, and I could tell by the look on his face that he'd been about to suggest the same thing.

I still consider that one of the worst days of my life so far, way worse even than all the times I peed my pants at school.

And speaking of wet pants, they weren't going to be a

problem for much longer. My parents had sort of hit Pause on the fight for me to use the bathroom at school while they were dealing with the whole soccer thing. As soon as that was all over, Mom got back to work on helping me win the right to use the bathroom. We decided to go over as many heads as we could and plead my case directly to the president! Mom posted a video on YouTube called "11-year-old transgender girl JAZZ, message to Obama." In it we did a quick recap of my life so far, and included a clip of me when I was younger saying:

I got in trouble for using the girls' bathroom, and I should have the right to use that bathroom. I'm not different from anybody else, and I can lock the door and make sure they don't walk in!

I doubt that Obama himself ever actually watched the video. (Or maybe he did . . . consider this foreshadowing!) However, things were finally turning around for me at school. After dealing with a few less-than-supportive principals, we now had a new, super-liberal principal named Ms. Percy. Ms. Reynolds had joked before she left when I started first grade that Mom—probably meaning *me*—had driven her into retirement!

And we'd had two other principals in the years after Ms. Reynolds left who hadn't done anything to improve my situation. Then Ms. Percy came in, and she made it clear from the start that she had my back no matter what. Not too much later the school board finally updated their policies to catch up with the regulation put out by the Office for Civil Rights of the US Department of Education that "prohibits discrimination against students on the basis of sex, gender identity, or sexual orientation."

Translation: I got to use the girls' bathroom! I could finally pee in peace.

Mom and I celebrate my Youth Courage Award from the Colin Higgins Foundation in New York City.

CHAPTER 11

"Just because someone's brain doesn't match their body, it doesn't mean they're a freak or a bad person! In fact, I think it means just the opposite. To me, kids like us are unique and special."

Winning the right to use the school bathrooms was a big deal, and toward the end of fifth grade something even more monumental happened—I became the youngest person to win the Youth Courage Award from the Colin Higgins Foundation!

Colin Higgins was this awesome writer and director who did some of the best classic movies from the seventies and eighties, like *Harold and Maude* and *9 to 5*. Before he tragically died from an AIDS-related illness in 1988, he set up a foundation to award grants to all kinds of LGBTQ organizations. The Youth Award goes to three different kids each year who, in the foundation's words, are "remarkable young people who refuse to be silenced by societal norms and demonstrate profound courage in the face of hardship, intolerance and bigotry based on sexual orientation, gender identity and national origin."

Whoa. I felt like all I was doing was living my normal life! I knew speaking on panels and doing interviews was helping people, but I never expected to get *rewarded* for it. I just liked the idea of spreading a positive message. Thanks to the love and support of my family, I knew how relatively easy my life had been compared to other transgender kids.

It was such a huge honor, and I was completely blown away by being chosen out of hundreds of people under consideration. The award was being given out in New York City at the TrevorLIVE fundraiser. The Trevor Project is a suicide prevention hotline for LGBTQ youth, and you can check out more about all the good stuff they do in the Resources section at the back of this book.

I was super comfortable in front of a crowd by this point, but I also knew that this experience was going to be different. I had to give a speech in front of about a thousand people. I spent over a week working with my parents, writing and rewriting it until I thought it was good enough, and then suddenly it was time to fly to New York. The event organizers put me through an hour of speech training, and I practiced in front of the mirror and my family. I had no idea what to wear, so before I'd left home I'd just grabbed the dress I'd worn to the twins' bar mitzvah.

Before the event, I walked a red carpet for the very first time, which was terrifying. I don't know how famous

people do it. There were so many bright lights and camera flashes and strangers sticking microphones in my face.
I quickly learned to say the same thing over and over so I
could keep moving down the line and get safely inside the
auditorium.

Once there, I couldn't get this one thing a reporter
had said to me out of my head. I knew it was meant to
be a compliment, but it was really bothering me for some
reason. He'd said, "You're transgender? I never would have
been able to tell!"

I was finally able to put my finger on it, and it's something that anyone who is meeting a transgender person
for the first time should keep in mind. Saying you "never
would have known" is actually very rude. Being surprised
that a person looks like the gender they are just reinforces
a stereotype that transgender people aren't usually attrac-
tive or able to pass, and worse, the stereotype that physical
appearances even matter. A person's true essence comes
from within!

I was getting so flustered that I almost didn't think I
could give my speech. Meeting some celebrities—like
Debra Messing, Stanley Tucci, and the band fun.—was a
nice distraction, but they all seemed like ordinary people I
might meet anywhere, so I didn't get starstruck or anything.

When it was finally time to give my speech, they had
to put a little crate behind the podium because I was too
short to reach the microphone. I took a deep breath, and
here's what I said:

Thank you so much to the Colin Higgins Foundation for honoring me with this award. This is the most exciting thing that has ever happened to me. And believe me, I have a pretty exciting life for an eleven-year-old girl! When my family and I first decided to share our story publicly we were all very nervous. At the time there were no young trans kids in the media. But after we shared our story on 20/20 with Barbara Walters, hundreds of other children and their families realized they were not alone. Families started listening to youth who were gender nonconforming, and more kids like me were allowed to be true to themselves.

It is so rewarding to inspire other children because let's face it, we are just kids, and all kids deserve to be happy. I have a motto: Everyone should be accepted for who they truly are. I've accomplished so much in the process of spreading this message. But compared to the plans I have in mind, there's still so much more to do.

It makes me sad knowing that so many transgender kids are bullied, depressed, and suicidal because they feel like they don't fit in. I want everyone to know that just because someone's brain doesn't match their body, it doesn't mean they're a freak or a bad person! In fact, I think it means just the opposite. To me, kids like us are unique and special, which I think is pretty cool.

During my life I have faced a lot of discrimination. I was banned from playing girls' soccer for two years, and that made me feel devastated. With the grant awarded to me by the Colin Higgins Foundation, I plan on paying it forward and donating the entire amount to our foundation, TransKids Purple Rainbow, so I can try my best to help other kids be as happy as I am right now. Before I go, I'd like to thank my family for the unconditional love you give me every day. I love you all so much.

As soon as I started talking up there, all my nervousness disappeared. I felt calm and strong, as if I'd been doing that sort of thing my whole life. Speaking out felt like what I was *meant* to do. Before that night, all my advocacy work had been done from the safety of my own home or at panels and conferences. But when I was speaking live in front of a massive banquet hall full of people, I felt a whole new energy running through me. I was connecting directly with everyone, and it brought out so much more emotion in me. I knew as soon as I walked off the stage that public speaking was going to become an even larger part of my life than I'd ever expected.

The next day, our whole family marched in the gay pride parade. The two other winners and I got to ride in a car while our families walked beside us, and my heart just about burst seeing millions of people cheering and showing their support. I knew I was on the right path.

All of this sounds very adult, right? Giving speeches and getting to be a guest of honor in a New York City parade are things that usually happen to people who have at least already gotten the right to vote. I'd never even flown on an airplane by myself. That changed the next month when I went to Camp Aranu'tiq, a camp specifically for transgender and gender nonconforming kids, for the first time.

"Aranu'tiq" is a word that comes from an indigenous population in Alaska. It describes a person who embodies both a male and a female spirit, and Aranu'tiq people are considered very special because it means they can see beyond a lot of the normal boundaries of the world and view things in all sorts of different ways. "Two-Spirit" is a similar Native American term.

Mom had originally found out about the camp through her online support network when I was younger, and the TransKids Purple Rainbow Foundation had already been sending the camp donations and providing scholarships for kids for a while. I'd never gone before because I'd been so focused on acting camp, but I finally lost faith that I'd ever get a real part after I couldn't even land the role of a completely made-up character in another production of *Alice in Wonderland*. For some reason, the director gave Tweedle Dee and Tweedle Dum a third brother named Tweedle Dah. If they weren't even going to toss me that pitiful bone, I was done.

I had actually gone to one overnight camp before, when I was nine. It was an acting camp that Ari had attended for years, but when I went, the director was nervous about letting me sleep in one of the girls' cabins. So they said if Mom came along with us and agreed to volunteer, they would give us a separate cabin of our own to sleep in. I was still officially assigned to a bunk, so I had a crew of girls to do all the daytime activities with, but at night Mom would have to come and drag me back to our own cabin, usually with me begging and pleading to be allowed to stay. It wasn't fair! It wasn't exactly the escape-from-adults experience that summer camp is supposed to be for kids.

On our very last night there, the counselors snuck me back into the girls' cabin after lights-out so that I could have at least one night as a regular camper. (One of the rule-breakers said, "Hey, it's our last night. What can they do, fire us?") I was so excited to stay up late with my should-have-been bunkmates, talking and gossiping and doing all the normal things campers are supposed to do after hours. And we did them all, but when we finally got tired and I climbed into the only empty bed, I discovered that no one had bothered to put sheets or a bedroll on it, so it was just me up against a scratchy, ratchet mattress with an itchy blanket on top! Sleeping with the other girls wasn't all that in the end, and I realized just how good I'd had it in my own private cabin with Mom.

When I boarded the plane for Camp Aranu'tiq, I felt more like a grown-up than I had speaking in front of hundreds of people at TrevorLIVE. I even remember thinking, *Wow! I am getting so old*, which is ridiculous because I was eleven.

Since it was a special occasion, I dressed up in my

favorite outfit for the trip (a gray tank top with navy polka dots and blue shorts with a sparkly belt) and brought a pink cheetah-print suitcase. The camp has two locations, one on the East Coast, in New England, and another on the West Coast, in California. The exact spots are kept secret to make sure everyone stays safe and their privacy is respected. Although the East Coast camp is closer to my home, it's held later in the summer after Florida schools have already started, so I had to fly out to California. The camp is run by a larger organization that also hosts a summer camp for kids with dwarfism, and another for kids who have craniofacial differences. The mission is to provide a safe experience for kids who might get made fun of at a regular summer camp. The cool thing is that the camps aren't full of workshops where you talk about what it's like being different—they're just regular camps with normal camp activities like swimming and rock climbing and singalongs. Naturally the kids end up bonding over their similar experiences out in the world, and all the great experiences at camp. The counselors' job is to just make sure everyone has fun.

My feelings on the plane about becoming an older woman got knocked down a few notches during our layover in Houston, where I had to spend the waiting time in a room full of other minors who were traveling by themselves. One Direction was just starting to become a huge deal at the time, and I eavesdropped on a bunch of Latina girls, trying to pick up on what they were saying with my basic Spanish vocabulary, until I realized their conversation mostly consisted of variations on "*Me gusta* One Direction!" I turned my attention instead to the bowls of free candy and loaded up for the next leg of the trip.

When I arrived in California, I was met at the gate by one of the counselors, whose job it was to drive me and a few other kids up to the camp. We collected three more first-time campers and all piled into the counselor's car, and I started talking with the others to get to know them. After we'd all told each other where we were from and how old we were, one boy named Kit asked, "So, do you all share the same deep dark secret that I have?"

His question startled me. "I do," I told him. "But for me, being transgender isn't a deep, dark secret. I don't mind telling people, I think I'm great just the way I am, and so are you."

I can't believe I just said that, I thought. It was a cool moment for me—I'd always felt great spreading a positive message in front of a roomful of strangers, but it was even better getting someone to feel good about who they are face to face. With the exception of the Philly conference, I hadn't really hung out with very many transgender kids before, and it was a much more satisfying feeling to connect with someone in person. It also made me kind of sad because I could tell Kit still felt some shame about his identity, but he relaxed almost right away after our conversation.

When we arrived at camp it turned out that we were

some of the first ones there. I met another counselor named Monica who offered to give me a tour of the place after we dropped off my bags in my bunk. She took me all around and showed me the cafeteria and the lake and the rock-climbing wall, and this weird little fenced-in area called the Gaga Pit, where kids get inside and knock little balls around at each other's feet. The goal is to not get hit below the knees—it's basically dodgeball but no one gets sucker-slammed in the face or stomach.

At one point during the tour Monica and I were walking down a dirt path when I tripped on a root and went sprawling face-first onto the ground. I scraped up my knee pretty bad, so that day she also showed me the infirmary—a place I would become very familiar with over the course of the week.

After I got bandaged up I went back to my room, where two of my cabinmates had arrived and were unpacking. Their names were Tia and Melinda, and they ended up becoming my two best friends for the week. I'd already met Melinda once before at the Philadelphia Trans-Health Conference when I was seven, and we'd been weirdly competitive when we were little kids, always trying to outdo each other with cartwheels or backflips. Now that we were older we put all that first-grade drama behind us. (Although she could be sort of disrespectful to the counselors, and that always frustrated me!)

I loved Tia immediately. She was two years older than

me and had been one of the very first campers ever at Aranu'tiq, and she was really into art and photography. She has an incredible sense of style but is very chill about it, not snobby like some people who are into fashion can be. There were around fifty kids total at the camp, and while we were friendly with everyone else, the three of us became an inseparable trio that went everywhere together.

Tia and Melinda weren't even grossed out when I puked up my dinner the very first night. The camp is in the mountains, and I'd never been at an elevation that high before. It messed with my stomach, and after eating a cheeseburger I spontaneously vomited all over the place and got sent to the infirmary for the second time. Thankfully, my body adjusted after a couple of days.

Just like at any other summer camp in the world, hormones were running pretty high, and Tia and Melinda landed boyfriends quickly. The two guys were already friends and had a third buddy named Aaron—it was expected that I would start dating him so we could hang out as one big group.

On the day they all introduced me to Aaron, he came striding over to where we were sitting cross-legged in the grass. I'm not sure if he normally acted that way, or maybe he was trying out some sort of new macho act because he had recently transitioned, but he had a very exaggerated swagger. His shoulders moved almost in time with his feet. It reminded me of a bad Justin Bieber impersonation.

"Hey, what's up," he said. It wasn't a question, and he gave me an all-over look. I was immediately uncomfortable. "How old are you?" he asked suspiciously.

"Um, eleven."

He looked at his two friends like they were insane. "Oh my God, you guys, I'm *fifteen*!" He turned around and strutted back the way he'd come.

Tia and Melinda started to apologize, but I waved them off. I was completely relieved. There were more interesting people to talk to, anyway.

There was another person in our cabin named Emory, who presented as a boy. None of us questioned why a guy had been placed in what was technically a girls' cabin—I guess we figured that since the camp was supportive of gender nonconforming kids it didn't really matter who slept where. Emory was really quiet and withdrawn, and midway through the week my bunkmates and I were all hanging out when we decided to try to get him to open up a bit. It turned out that he had no idea why his mom had sent him to Camp Aranu'tiq! When we explained that we were all transgender, and what that meant exactly, it was like a huge lightbulb went on.

"I feel like I'm a girl inside, too!" Emory exclaimed. "So *that's* why my mom sent me here!"

We spent the next couple of hours telling Emory all our stories, about how all of us had felt alone or struggled at some point. By the end of the conversation, Emory decided she wanted to go by the name Remy, and we all donated pieces of our clothing for her to wear and take home with her. The difference in Remy's demeanor was a total turnaround. She became super friendly and outgoing, and it was so powerful to see her come into her own within a matter of hours of being surrounded by a support system. It's incredible what even just a little kindness and acceptance can do for a person.

The rest of the week flew by. We took arts and crafts classes, performed little skits in a drama class, and played a whole lot of Gaga, which I was pretty great at thanks to years of soccer. I loved our writing class and wrote a story I was really proud of. It explained in detail my grand philosophy of life, and how everything and everyone is connected. Just kidding. I think it was about a tree or something.

On the last day of camp, the counselors threw us a big party in the cafeteria. I was dancing with Tia and Melinda and their boyfriends, as well as this younger girl I'd gotten friendly with named Olivia. We were spazzing out near the speakers when, as if in slow motion, I saw Olivia stumble and start to fall to the ground. I dove forward to catch her before she hit the floor and managed to rescue her, but in the process I sliced my leg open from the top of my thigh to just above my knee on the corner of one of the speakers! I ended camp as I had begun it—getting a bloody leg cleaned up by the nurse in the infirmary.

When I stepped off the plane back in Florida the next

day, my mom flipped out—I was so banged up she thought I'd been in a car accident and no one had bothered to call her!

After I calmed her down and we drove back home, I told her everything that had happened over the past week. As I talked, it started to dawn on me just how cool the whole thing had really been. The experience had been so beautifully *ordinary*. Everyone had been able to express themselves with zero judgments. It had positively affected so many of the kids—the ones who were shy for the first day or two were running around laughing hysterically with a whole posse of new friends by the end of the week. I thought again about how lucky I was to have such a relatively conflict-free life. Every single transgender child deserves to have the same, and I'll always be reminded of the positive power of Camp Aranu'tiq whenever I glance down at the fourteen-inch scar on my leg.

Barbara Walters and my family, after she interviewed
me for the second time when I was eleven.

CHAPTER 12

*"I'm here for you. I'm fighting for you.
That's what I do. Every day I hope you
can feel safe and happy."*

When Ari first went to middle school, my mom had entered her in a lottery for our town's best charter school, which offered a much more progressive education than any of the other nearby options. Ari got in, and once one family member is accepted, all of their siblings get an automatic ticket, too. The school runs sixth through twelfth grade, with sixth through eighth as middle school.

When my mom first went to talk to the administration to find out if it would be a safe place for me, she immediately felt relieved when she saw a poster in an office window advocating transgender rights. Score! Best of all, the principal promised her that I'd be allowed to use the girls' bathroom, so we didn't have to worry about that at all. The only thing that sucked was that Casey wasn't going to be at the same school with me, but we swore to each other that we'd stay best friends.

I'd been calling myself Jazz at camp and in public for all of my advocacy work for so long that I decided to finally make it my official name. I'd actually wanted to do it as far back as elementary school, but Ms. Reynolds hadn't let me because she said it wasn't "a real name," whatever that means. Anything can be a name! I felt like Jazz fit me, and it was time to make it permanent. On the first day of school I was recovering from a cold and had lost my voice, so every time a teacher called me Jaron in class I'd croak, "It's Jaaazzz," in a deep, froggy monster voice. Not a very glamorous beginning to my new life.

I started making friends immediately. In art class, I ran into a girl named Sophie who I'd vaguely known in elementary school. She was very outgoing—she came right up to me and said she knew I was transgender.

"I really look up to you and I want to be your friend," she said.

Done and done. I met a few other girls, including one named Renee who I knew from soccer. I was able to avoid the universal crushing humiliation of trying to figure out where to sit in the cafeteria on the first day of a new school when someone else I knew from elementary school saw Renee and me and waved us over to her table.

For the first few weeks, I thought everything was going to be great. I loved my new social group. I'd always been pretty upbeat and confident in elementary school, but in middle school that attitude finally seemed to really work in terms of making friends. One day while I was talking with a big group of people in the hallway, both guys and girls, it hit me over the head—I was *popular.* I'd never experienced anything like it. I wasn't trying to hide the fact that I was transgender—my closest friends all knew. But I wasn't exactly advertising it, either.

Going ice-skating on Friday nights was a really big deal in our grade, and one week Sophie and I organized a huge get-together of friends, including a bunch of boys. I was taking a break from skating and resting against the wall when one of the guys came gliding up to me and said, "I know someone who has a crush on you!"

"Who?!"

"Can't tell you," he called over his shoulder while skating away.

I looked around at all the guys we'd invited. Some of them were really cute, and I started to get excited. But I couldn't figure out a way to find out which one liked me! I had a hunch that it was a guy named Sam, who had been talking to me a lot, but I hoped it was someone different. Something about Sam rubbed me the wrong way, but I couldn't figure out exactly what.

In the end, my secret admirer was an easy discovery. It was the guy who texted me out of nowhere after getting my number from someone else. His name was Jason, and he was good-looking but way shorter than me. I didn't mind. I don't think I would have picked him out of a crowd as someone I'd be interested in going after, but the fact that he liked me was enough for me to like him back. We started to text a lot at night and then began talking in school. The more I got to know him, the more I liked him.

I was up front with him early on, and came out to him as transgender via text:

ME: I wanted to tell you that I'm transgender, which means that I was a boy but became a girl so I have a girl brain and a boy body.

He wrote back immediately.

JASON: But you have a girl body, right?

I got nervous about clarifying that question further. I'd already spelled it out for him, so I sent him a link to a You-Tube video I'd made when I was younger that gave a much more detailed description about being transgender. He still didn't fully understand.

JASON: That's a cute video. So what parts of a boy do you have?

ME: The P word.

He wrote back that he accepted me for who I was, so I thought everything was going to be okay, but he suddenly stopped talking to me. I tried to shake it off and not let it get to me, but not long after I told him, a girl I was friendly with named Julia stopped me in the hallway between classes.

"Listen, I think you should know something," she started to say, but then began squirming and looking uncomfortable.

"What?"

"I . . . I overheard Sam talking about you with some of the other boys. He called you . . ." She lowered her voice. "A chick with a dick."

That nasty, horrible phrase again. I thanked her for letting me know, and as I walked down the hallway I realized that the boys who usually smiled at me or said hi were all turning away from me fast, pretending to be absorbed with something really important deep inside their lockers.

I was so hurt, and I wasn't used to feeling bruised by insults. My usual defense—confidence—deserted me, and I felt vulnerable and alone.

Along with some girls, every single one of my male friends, including Jason, deserted me within a day. They were scared that if they were seen with me, or God forbid *dated* me, they'd be considered gay. Realizing that that kind of ignorant thought process was behind Jason ditching me was what got me back on my feet. If a boy doesn't like me because I'm transgender, I know he isn't right for me to begin with. End of story.

I know it would have been easy for me to stay really

bummed out and wallow in misery, but being transgender is such a huge part of my identity that it overrules any romantic feelings I have for someone else. I can see how some people might think that's just a form of self-preservation—a sort of defensive wall I've built up to protect myself from getting hurt. I really don't think that's it, though. I'm genuinely proud of who I am, and someone who can't see a person's soul beyond their body isn't worth getting upset about. If anything, experiencing that kind of discrimination just pumps me up and makes me more determined to speak out and try to educate the world. When I told my mom everything that had gone down, she ended up getting more upset about it than I was!

Sophie and some other girlfriends stuck by my side, and their friendship meant more to me than any dumb boy's attention or rejection. The ones in our group who hadn't known about me were basically like, "Oh, you're transgender? That's cool, let's go get pizza."

Not long after I returned to school from winter break, a second Barbara Walters special on transgender kids that I'd shot with her earlier that year aired. My parts of the show were basically just the two of us catching up with my life since she'd last seen me. The project had been in the works for a while, and they'd even sent a camera crew to Trevor-LIVE to see me accept the Colin Higgins Youth Courage Award and march in the gay pride parade to gather extra footage. While I'd been in New York, I'd met with Barbara and gotten to sing the song from *Cinderella* for her again.

(I was happy for the do-over, since I hadn't been sick that time and actually sounded good!)

The producers had also sent a camera crew to our house in Florida to shoot some day-to-day-life stuff, and even though Jason didn't matter to me at all, it was still a little hard to watch one scene where the cameras caught my whole text exchange with him when I came out as trans. I had mentioned to a producer that I had been texting with a boy recently and he asked if they could record it. I hadn't really stopped to think about what would happen if Jason ended up having a negative reaction. It wasn't that I was upset about being reminded of him specifically; it was more that it was frustrating to be reminded that many boys can be pretty narrow-minded.

I was nervous about going to school the day after the show premiered, but I worried for nothing. A lot of kids approached me and said they'd watched the special and that they had my back, so the show ended up being sort of a friend detector. The school's dean of discipline, Mr. Lorre, called me into his office and told me that if I ever needed any help or someone to talk to, he would stand by my side. It felt so great to have that extra support from the administration. And Sam even apologized for saying mean things about me. I appreciated that he made the effort, but I didn't think it was very sincere. I got the distinct feeling that he was suddenly interested in being my friend only because I had been on TV, so I didn't bother continuing to talk to him after that.

One day our class went on a field trip to see a play called *Eureka*, which was all about this girl who's having trouble understanding math, and the night before a big test she's visited by the ghosts of Albert Einstein and Pythagoras. (Don't ask.)

Just before it started, I heard a boy sitting directly in front of me start to talk to the kid next to him.

"Have you heard of this boy in the sixth grade that thinks he's a girl? I think his name is Jazz or something."

"Hello!" I said as loudly as I could. "I'm sitting right behind you. Don't talk crap about me!"

I was furious and was not about to put up with it. I stood up and waved a teacher over.

"These kids are saying ignorant things about me, and I think it's very disrespectful," I said. She promised to take care of it and moved them to different seats.

I think a lot of kids feel too scared to confront someone who is saying mean things about them. It's so important to defend yourself. Be proud about speaking back and not shying away from the situation, *as long as you feel safe.* If I had been alone on a sidewalk and heard those two guys talking in front of me, I might have reacted differently—or not at all. While it's always good to stick up for yourself, it's more important to assess the situation first and make sure there isn't any chance of getting physically hurt.

The homicide rate for transgender women in America hit a historic high in 2015, according to the Human Rights Campaign, even with all the current support and visibility.

Almost all of them were women of color, and the number killed was twenty-one as of November 2015—that's basically two people a month, and the real number is likely to be even higher due to unreported cases. Worldwide it's much worse: Between 2008 and 2014, there were 1,731 reported murders. That's really terrifying, and a huge reason why I continue to be a public advocate and keep speaking out. Change happens through understanding, and one of my biggest hopes is that our next generation of kids will grow up in a world with more compassion.

Modeling one of my mermaid tails.
I'm still obsessed with mermaids.

CHAPTER 13

"Different is the new normal."

Have you ever heard of the Truth Game? Hopefully you haven't, and hopefully my telling this story won't inspire anyone else to try it. Trust me, it doesn't lead anywhere good.

The idea behind the Truth Game is that it can make friends grow stronger. Before you start, you have to swear an oath that neither person will be offended by anything the other one says. You then take turns saying everything you like and don't like about each other. TERRIBLE IDEA, right? Whoever invented this game is a sadist dedicated to destroying friendships.

Sophie and I played it one afternoon when I was twelve. Of course we started out with all the sweet, kind, good stuff, like how much we liked each other's hair. Then things got real. I told her I thought she took her jokes too far sometimes and that they could even be rude and insulting. She told me she thought I rubbed it in her face that I did really well in school and sports.

In retrospect these seem like tiny problems that could be easily resolved. Instead, talking about them in this stupid game almost wrecked our friendship. We got in a huge fight and stopped speaking to each other, and it couldn't have happened at a worse moment, because it was right around the time that depression entered my life.

It wasn't the fight that caused it. And I knew it didn't have anything to do with me being transgender, either. I felt fine on that front. But almost overnight I developed an overwhelming sense that nothing mattered in life.

I stopped talking to all my friends and would find myself banging my head repeatedly against walls, usually in the bathroom at school. Whenever someone walked in on me and asked me why I was doing it, I'd ignore them. I didn't want to talk to anyone. I'd always done so well in school and I loved to learn new things, but all my classes suddenly became boring—to the point where I wanted to scream in frustration.

These new feelings scared me, and I tried to rationalize what was happening by telling myself that in order to move forward in life, a person needs to find purpose. I'd always found motivation in being an advocate, in pushing myself to get straight As, and in playing my best on the soccer field. Somehow my love of all of those things had slipped through my fingers. The world felt like a meaning-less void. I was stumbling through it with no direction, and worse, no desire to find one.

My parents grew really worried about me and even alerted the school about my state of mind. Depression runs in my mom's side of the family, and she had experienced postpartum depression after giving birth to me that con-tinued for years, so she recognized the symptoms. She took me to a psychiatrist, who diagnosed me with both depres-sion and anxiety and prescribed antidepressants.

They didn't work. Antidepressants aren't a sudden, magical cure-all. Since everyone's body chemistry is differ-ent, it usually takes some time to find the right one or the right combination, as well as the correct dosage. To make things worse, I started to notice that the girls in my grade were developing breasts. I felt so left behind—I'd been des-perate to grow boobs ever since I was a little kid. I'd man-aged to come so far as a girl, but suddenly my life seemed to screech to a halt while the rest of the world sped up around me. This situational depression on top of the sad-ness I was already feeling thanks to some bad genes got to be too much, and Mom took me to both an endocrinologist and Dr. Marilyn for advice.

They thought the hormone blockers might be depriv-ing me of something essential that my body needed to bal-ance itself out. As I have said, not every trans girl has access to this hormone therapy. And some choose not to take it.

But for those who have decided to take estrogen, there's no set-in-stone age to start the treatment, although many doctors won't prescribe it until a patient turns sixteen. I was only twelve, but we made the choice to go for it. One possible side effect of estrogen is that it can cause a person to become moody, so there was a chance that the plan would backfire and make things worse for me. I couldn't imagine feeling worse than I already did, though, so we decided to move forward.

On March 6, 2012, I got my first dose of estrogen. I think a lot of transgender people who decide to take hormones remember the date of their first course. It felt like a second birthday, because I knew my body was finally going to start catching up with my brain.

The plan worked. We also made an adjustment in my antidepressant dosage, and I gradually felt my spirits start to rise after a couple of weeks. Even better, my boobs started to grow! At first they felt like two little bug bites, then quickly turned into what seemed like two seeds under my skin. I'd been obsessively researching the stages of breast development for years and knew all the normal signs. I didn't mind the soreness I felt because I knew the ache was leading to something huge in my life. (Not huge *boobs*— finally experiencing a female body!)

I continued to keep to myself at school for the most part during this period. I didn't tell my friends I was depressed, so they had no idea why I was so withdrawn. Casey was the one person I had told and still felt genuinely close to, but soon I started to let other people back into my life. Sophie and I formed a truce since we were on the school's soccer team together, but it would be a while before we became as close as we had been before. I generally kept people at a distance while I adjusted to my new hormones and emerged from my sadness. One thing that really helped move me forward was writing in my journal, and I recently found this entry, which I think is a pretty good example of where my head was at around this time:

> *The sea is a multitude of raindrops. In my life, I will make mistakes. I will have moments where I'm a good person, and moments where I'm a bad person. I will make wrong decisions. I will make right decisions. In the end, it is about finding happiness and creating a ripple effect on this world. Your destiny is controlled with every path you journey on.*

A lot of writers and artists have experienced depression, so I think it makes sense that sixth grade is when I also started to learn a lot more about art and experiment with different tools. Art became a visual way for me to express emotions that were sometimes too hard to put into words. I'd never stopped drawing since I was a little kid, but my work had evolved from vaginas and big boobs to mermaids with vaginas and big boobs. I'd start their scales just below their genitals, so it sort of looked like they'd gotten pantsed—or whatever the mermaid version of getting your pants pulled down on the playground is. Tailed?

More important, I started to work on realistic portraits of people. I'd first started drawing faces when I was around eight, but I began to concentrate on capturing more of a person's essence by focusing on intricate details in the eyes. I'd search the Internet for faces that had a certain beauty or expression I wanted to re-create, and learned about shading to help create the illusion of depth on a two-dimensional surface. I experimented more with charcoals and color. One of my pictures, a charcoal and pastel portrait of a girl with a flower in her hair, even got selected by my art teacher to be presented in a gallery downtown!

I kept coming back to mermaids, though, and started to become obsessed with the idea of trying to create a very realistic tail. When I was younger I used to sew mermaid tail costumes all the time. I'd slip one on and swim around in our pool a few times until it fell apart, and then make a new one to replace it. Now that I was older, I wanted something that looked and felt more real, and I figured if Hollywood special effects companies could create mermaid tails, I should be able to teach myself to make them, too.

I began doing research online and discovered an entire community of grown-ups who loved mermaids as much as I did. I joined a chat group made up of people who built tails as a hobby, and even though I wasn't even a teenager yet, they welcomed me right in. I told them I wanted to try to make my first tail over the summer once school was over, and everyone was so supportive and offered me tips they'd learned from creating their own.

As you can probably imagine, making a realistic mermaid tail is a pretty intense process, not to mention an expensive one. My parents agreed to help me pay for the materials I'd need to buy, like buckets of silicone and fiberglass resin, if I promised to work harder at connecting with school and the world in general.

The hormones definitely helped me with that. On the soccer field all of us girls would compare our emerging boobs. On the one hand, those talks made me feel like part of the group, since I had my own boobs starting to pop out and could participate. On the other hand, I knew that some of the girls were starting to get their periods, and that was a rite of passage I was never going to be able to share with them. Sometimes one would ask if I'd gotten mine yet, and I'd have to remind them that it was impossible for me. I'd tell them, "Hello, I have a D, remember?!"

As the school year ended, I slowly gathered all the materials I'd need for my mermaid project, and I got to work on the first day of summer vacation. Casey and I reunited and she helped me every step of the way. I won't go over every single tiny detail, but I do want to share the basics so you can get a sense of how involved the process is.

The first thing I had to do was sketch out what I wanted the tail to look like, and for my first attempt I chose green, with blue highlights along the sides and hints of yellow down the middle. I bought a diver's monofin, which is like a regular pair of flippers but fused into one piece. The fluke—that's the wide, flat part of the tail—gets built around this, so you have something to slip your feet into inside the tail, making it easier to swim with.

I traced the outline of the monofin on paper, and then sketched out the shape of my tail over that. (I messed up the first time because I didn't create an exact mirror image of each half, which screwed up the seal.)

Next I used clay to sculpt around the fin and create the shape of the fluke, and Casey wrapped the lower half of my body in plaster to form a mold. Then I had to make scales, which presented a problem. I couldn't figure out an easy way to create thousands (no joke) of perfectly even little half-circles that would look like fish scales. Genius struck when I was cruising through a craft store website and came across a bunch of tiny discs in the shape of soccer balls that I guess were meant to be used as scrapbooking décor. I ordered a ton of them, spent days gluing them side by side in overlapping rows on a piece of cardboard, and then created a silicone mold out of that sheet to place over the body cast. Then I poured liquid silicone into the mold, waited for it to set, repeated the process, and then sealed the two pieces together and painted them.

There are a million other steps that are too detailed and boring to get into here, but the instructions are online if you're really interested. The important thing is that the project brought me back to myself and out of my depression. It gave me a sense of purpose and direction. Casey and I grew even closer with all our mistakes and little successes along the way. I quickly became convinced that I wanted to build a career making and selling mermaid tails. I figured I could donate a huge portion of the sales to TransKids Purple Rainbow Foundation.

Once the tail was completed, I took my first swim in it. When I'm underwater, I always hear the same music playing in my head. It's a very simple melody that's at odds with the strength I feel in my lower body as I swim from one side of the pool to the other.

I felt so powerful inside my mermaid tail, but my real body was starting to rebel against me from the hormones. My depression had evened out, but the estrogen began to make me gain a little bit of weight, and I grew really self-conscious—not good, when a big part of my intended career path included modeling my tail creations in a shell bra.

Feeling self-conscious about how I looked had another impact on me as well. I was continuing to speak out and give interviews in order to spread a message of self-acceptance to other LGBTQ kids across the world, and the double standard messed with my head—if I didn't like my own body, how was I supposed to convince anyone else to love theirs? I know many other girls struggle with body issues—sadly, it's just a huge part of our society, thanks to impossible ideals shown in magazines and movies and on TV. I thought I was a stronger person and could rise above it, and it freaked me out to realize how much my extra weight bothered me. I couldn't figure out how to take my own advice.

Feeling bad about my body didn't get any better when Sophie stopped by the house that summer to say hi. I couldn't stop staring at her chest—her boobs had basically exploded. She'd gone from an A cup to a B cup overnight! She even pulled up her shirt to show them to me.

"Crazy, right?" she said.

"Crazy," I said, nodding. More like crazy jealous.

Laverne Cox is such an inspiration for me.
She's also talented, sweet, and beautiful!

CHAPTER 14

"Would you rather have a dead son or a living daughter?"

On the first day of seventh grade I kept hearing the same question over and over again: "Where were you all summer?"

Which was good, because talking about my mermaid tail project kept me from feeling too frustrated about being back in school. I still did all my homework and got 100s on all my tests, but none of the subjects I was studying, with the exception of art, seemed important to my life in any way. I'd just spent three months teaching myself a *real* skill that I loved. (To be fair to my teachers, I did have to use some math to figure it all out.)

Art class was great, with one exception. We had assigned seating and I was with two girls and a guy, Jenna, Anna, and Ray. One day we were all talking while working on our projects when I heard Ray ask Anna, "Do you know about It? *It* is so annoying."

"Yeah, It is so stupid," she said.

"Totally," I agreed, thinking they were talking about the evil clown that Stephen King made up in his book *It*. "The movie is kind of lame, but I heard someone's doing a remake!"

From that day on the three of them constantly talked about It and said really mean things about It, like that It was idiotic. I quickly began to suspect that *I* was It. I confronted Jenna and she swore up and down that they weren't talking about me, but it seemed really suspicious that the three of them would harbor that much dislike for so long over an imaginary monster.

So I ignored them. I had more important things going on, like looking forward to turning thirteen that October. But once my birthday came, I didn't feel any different. There was no big magical "Ooooh, I'm a teenager now" sensation. It's possible that I was feeling something deeper inside, though—at the start of the year I had begun to draw a bunch of Disney characters on my bedroom wall, but I abandoned the project. Maybe somewhere in the back of my head I understood that I really was growing up. Not that there's anything wrong with Winnie the Pooh, but I didn't need to look at him every day.

At least other people started to see me as getting older. Ari bought me my first bra that truly belonged to me—I'd been wearing her old ones. It was from Victoria's Secret and was hot pink. At the time it was my absolute favorite. (Unfortunately—and fortunately—I've now grown out of it.)

I liked how it looked when I first tried it on, but my other reaction was *I wish I had more cleavage.* I didn't feel like I was developing fast enough. I started watching You-Tube tutorials by drag queens who showed how to create the illusion of cleavage by squeezing your chest together and adding contour lines with makeup. Casey was in the same boat I was and we'd text each other photos of our attempts. Some tries came out pretty good under certain lighting, but nothing was strong enough that I ever felt comfortable leaving the house with the results.

I made some new friends that year, like a girl named Alana who was also on my soccer team, but in general I wasn't feeling super social, so for the most part I kept to myself, with the exception of Casey outside school. We still hung out constantly, and that Halloween I used everything I'd learned about making mermaid tails to create custom latex masks for us to wear—I went as a zombie Santa and she was a zombie elf.

The next month, *Out* magazine honored me as one of their "Out 100." I was the youngest person to ever be included on the list, and I was incredibly grateful, but it didn't affect my day-to-day life at all. As far as I knew, no one in my middle school was even aware it had happened, and I wasn't about to bring attention to it. I preferred to fly under the radar and work on my big master mermaid plan.

I started my YouTube channel specifically to promote

my tail business, which I had decided to name Purple Rainbow Tails, after TransKids Purple Rainbow Foundation. I knew I'd have to raise money to really get going with it, so I started a crowdfunding account on Indiegogo to earn some start-up cash. I reached my goal way faster than I thought I would, and at the same time someone who works for Weeki Wachee Springs contacted me. They wanted me to make two tails for their annual mermaid calendar!

Weeki Wachee is this park in Florida famous for its live mermaid shows, which take place underwater in a natural spring. It started as a tiny roadside attraction in 1947, and back then the road was so small and rarely traveled that whenever the girls who played the mermaids would hear a car coming, they'd run out and try to lure the family in to see them do their swim routines. In the 1950s and 1960s, the Weeki Wachee mermaids were world-famous. The place has been kind of a cult road trip destination ever since. Naturally, when I was a kid I was totally obsessed with it, so it was a big deal for me that Weeki Wachee wanted me to get involved with them.

The only problem was that I had promised the largest donor on Indiegogo that I would make them a tail as well, so suddenly I was faced with trying to make three tails at once, while balancing school and soccer. To top things off, I was in the process of working with a woman named Jessica Herthel on a children's picture book!

My mom has known Jessica for years. She's a lawyer and used to be the director of the Stonewall National Education Project, which develops LGBTQ educational materials for schools around the country. Mom had worked with her on a bunch of different projects for our school district, and Jessica had originally approached Mom toward the end of sixth grade to see if I'd be willing to work on a kids' book about being transgender, because there were none out there. It had never even occurred to me that really little kids didn't have a simple book that explained what it meant to be trans. More important, it suddenly felt worrying to me that there wasn't a book for a little trans kid to see a reflection of himself or herself in. I would have given anything as a child to see someone like me represented in a bedtime story. Plus I knew it was a great opportunity to educate nontrans people.

Jessica came up with the basic outline, and I gave her a lot of thoughts and ideas I'd had as a kid. She had gotten advice from publishers who wanted us to write the book with some sort of setting or activity, like *Jazz Goes to the Zoo!* But we felt like the best way to do the book was to be straightforward. We didn't need to disguise what we had to say, like some sort of sneak attack lesson delivered while distracting a kid with a cute picture of a lion. There's so much to write about being transgender that it was hard enough to narrow everything down into just a few short sentences that were kid-friendly and easy to understand. Penguin signed the book up (coincidentally, on November 20—the Transgender Day of Remembrance, which honors people who have lost their lives to antitrans violence).

Penguin helped us find an amazing illustrator in England named Shelagh McNicholas to draw the pictures. All proceeds that normally would go to the authors instead go straight to TransKids Purple Rainbow Foundation.

Little did I know at the time that a few years later a school in a small town in Wisconsin would cancel a reading of the book because they were threatened with a federal lawsuit! After the school's principal sent a note to parents letting them know about the reading, a right-wing organization wrote a scary letter saying our book was about a "psychological and moral disorder." They threatened to sue the teachers and staff, and the school had to back down.

There was a happy ending, though! The residents of Mount Horeb, Wisconsin, rallied together and hosted their own reading at their library. The Human Rights Campaign even flew Jessica in to read, and close to six hundred people showed up! I was lucky enough to get to thank them all in an article I wrote for the Milwaukee *Journal Sentinel*.

So, yeah, even without knowing about the future controversy the book would spark, things were pretty busy that school year. Somehow I managed to balance most of it, with the exception of the tail for my biggest Indiegogo supporter. That ended up getting delayed, and I felt awful about it. To make things worse, I hadn't asked my parents' permission before starting the tail fundraising and making the promise to create tails for large donors online. They were pretty mad when they found out because they knew I was in over my head, and I ended up having to refund one donor's money. The downside to being interested in so many different things in the world is that it can sometimes lead to projects I don't finish.

That spring the Gay & Lesbian Alliance Against Defamation contacted my mom and asked if I'd be willing to speak at their annual GLAAD Media Awards event, which honors magazines, movies, advertising, TV shows, and all sorts of other media for representing LGBT people in a positive way.

I knew it was going to be a big ceremony, and I agonized over what to say. I wouldn't have a whole lot of time, so I needed to keep it short. Here's what I went with:

> *It's amazing to be here tonight, representing all the LGBTQ kids and teens out there. I just want them to know that it's okay to step out of your shadows and just be who you are. Just be true to yourself and express yourself.*

Before my speech, I once more needed a box to be brought out so I wasn't peeking over the top of the podium. I stood between actress Elle Fanning and Alex Newell from *Glee*. A lot of people asked me if I was nervous, and I was a little, about speaking in front of three thousand people, but not about meeting the celebrities. Being around famous people still didn't faze me at all. They are people, just like anyone else.

Quick side note about that, though: It *was* pretty cool

to meet Laverne Cox—the transgender actress from *Orange Is the New Black*. Not so much because she's a star, but because she's such an incredible role model, and everything she has to say about transgender rights is always so perfectly on point. She stopped me to talk when I was at Logo TV's Trailblazer Honors the following summer. She was everything you'd imagine her to be—sweet, kind, and funny—but when anyone says they're proud of me, like she did, I get flustered. I don't know what to say except thank you, because I really don't feel like I'm doing anything special. I just live my normal life, trying to stay on top of homework, sports commitments, and my mermaid tail business.

Okay, maybe that last one isn't so normal.

The weirdest part of the GLAAD Awards night was meeting former president Bill Clinton and his daughter, Chelsea. I could tell my mom was freaking out. I mean, he used to be the president! Again, though, to me he was just a normal person. Both he and Chelsea were polite and said, "Nice to meet you," but then none of us knew what to say and we all sort of stood there in awkward silence until Chelsea complimented the dress I was wearing. (We actually almost didn't end up getting to meet them because Betty White pushed ahead of us in the line of people waiting to say hi!)

Jennifer Lawrence came up to me to talk a little later, and that was pretty neat. Jennifer told me she thought it was cool how my mom was supportive of me, and when we started talking about *The Hunger Games*, she told me she was nothing like Katniss Everdeen in real life.

I could relate. In my real life, I didn't feel like that girl up on the stage who everyone else saw and kept calling brave. I believe the truly brave ones are all the transgender kids out there in the world who go about their daily lives without the kind of love and encouragement I have—the kids who have to constantly talk themselves out of suicidal thoughts and face harassment and violence at school and even at home. Every time I get too wrapped up in this thought process and start feeling bad, Mom reminds me that it's brave to simply be a face and a voice for trans kids who don't have support or a platform. I'm always happy to do that, but I'm still not exactly comfortable with the word "brave." I'll take "confident" because I know I am, and if that's enough to help people, I'll keep on talking.

All the media attention I'd gotten made my Instagram account grow faster and faster, and I had already gained a few thousand followers. I thought it would be funny to post a photo of me with Jennifer Lawrence when I got back home, since she's such a big deal for my generation thanks to *The Hunger Games*. My status in the eyes of my classmates changed overnight. Total strangers started coming up to me in the hallways and squealing about the fact that I'd met her. Every time someone asked what she was like, I'd shrug my shoulders and tell them, "She's nice. And normal."

All right, I admit it. I'm not *totally* immune to the whole celebrity thing. But not for the reasons you might think. It's not like I'm worshipping them; it's just so surreal and disorienting to be talking somewhere like the GLAAD Awards and look down into the audience and see Leonardo DiCaprio, Drew Barrymore, and Tobey Maguire staring back up at me. It feels like the laws of the universe have been flipped—I'm supposed to be the one watching *them*!

One thing I definitely was still watching at the time was my weight. I was really unhappy with my belly, so I'd do quickie fixes like the Military Diet, which lets you eat things like hot dogs and ice cream for three days but you still lose pounds. It's horribly unhealthy, I know, but it would work—for about the same amount of time as the diet itself, and then the weight would come right back.

I decided soccer wasn't enough exercise, so I joined the school tennis team, but at first it was the soccer situation all over again. The coach liked me, but I wasn't allowed to play with the girls. I could practice with them, but I had to sit out each game until the Florida High School Athletic Association confirmed that I had been diagnosed by a medical professional as having gender dysphoria. They actually had an existing sports inclusion policy, which is cool, but it had never been used before and we had to file a ton of paperwork first, like letters from my pediatrician and Dr. Marilyn. Overall they were way more understanding than the state soccer association, though, and I only had to miss three games before I was allowed to play.

Pretty eventful school year, right? I made the National Junior Honors Society, too. (Sorry, I had to sneak that in. I don't like bragging, but academics are huge to me—and I know how important they are to my mom and dad!)

There was one lame thing that happened, though. On the last day of school, I got my yearbook back from Jenna, one of the girls from my art class, after I asked her to sign it. She scribbled her name and then wrote: "It is you."

I knew it, I thought, utterly dismayed. I felt myself starting to get more and more upset before I forced myself to get my priorities in order. I had no time in my life for that kind of lame bullying, so I decided to turn their mean nickname into a compliment. Most people would love to be an It Girl!

Not everyone has my ability to let go of bad things, and as summer started to get under way I got a really heart-breaking reminder about that.

I was on vacation with my family in Virginia Beach when Mom got an email through the TransKids Purple Rainbow Foundation website that shook her to the core. Dad gathered us all together into one hotel room and read the letter to us, because he thought it was really important that we all hear what it said.

The message was from a mother who reminded me a lot of my own parents. She had a child named Edward, who was drawn to girly things like princess dresses and dolls from the very beginning. The family happily provided these things on birthdays and holidays because they saw how happy they made Edward.

By the time puberty hit, Edward had done enough

research on the Internet to understand that she was transgender, and told her parents that she was a girl trapped in a boy's body. Like my own parents, they immediately set out to find a doctor who could help, but they lived in a country that didn't accept being transgender was something a child could experience. The common belief among their medical community was that only adults could experience gender dysphoria.

They were eventually able to find a psychiatrist who was willing to see Edward as she transitioned to Angeline, but the doctor drew the line at prescribing any sort of hormone blockers or estrogen. So while Angeline socially transitioned, she suffered through male puberty, including growing facial hair and developing a deep voice.

She was teased mercilessly at school, and even hurt physically. Her parents tried to intervene, but Angeline was worried that would make things even worse among her peers, so she stopped telling her family when she experienced abuse.

As her sadness worsened, her psychiatrist prescribed antidepressants, but the medication didn't work. Angeline hanged herself in her family's garage and left a note asking that her life savings, a little over one thousand dollars, be left to TransKids Purple Rainbow Foundation to help continue the fight to make sure no kid ever feels that suicide is their only option.

This letter was beyond devastating. Without her child in her life, Angeline's mother described herself as an amputee, and she said that the family's hearts were all still bleeding.

At first none of us knew what to say, sitting there all piled up on the hotel beds. But soon we began to talk about advocacy work, and how important it is that we keep it up. We'd gotten many letters before through the foundation from kids who had been contemplating suicide, but they had always been able to talk themselves out of it when they thought of my family and me. Whenever I read one of those letters I felt wonderful inside, but Angeline made me realize that there were still so many kids out there to help. She had known about us, read our messages, seen our videos, but they hadn't been enough to save her. I knew it wasn't my fault, but I couldn't help feeling angry and frustrated that there wasn't something more I could have done.

There's a very common saying when it comes to spreading any kind of message of hope, and I've even said it myself: "If I can help just one person, it will all be worth it."

Yes, that's technically true. But after Angeline, I want to reach everyone.

One of the best parts of attending the Philadelphia
Trans-Health Conference is reconnecting with
friends from all over the country, including our
close friends Mary and Chris.

CHAPTER 15

"I've experienced bullying and isolation, but in the end all of these obstacles have made me a better person, a stronger person, a person with pride."

When society tells you that genitalia dictate your gender, you better believe that many transgender kids are going to study up on what is or isn't between our legs. I think a lot of us learn about sex early, because we spend so much time researching and talking about the human body. And like any other place where you gather a bunch of teenagers together on an overnight trip, the Philadelphia Trans-Heath Conference was a breeding ground for sex talk.

Quick side note for any parents out there reading this—do NOT let me saying this deter you from letting your kid attend if you're considering it. It's really healthy for trans teens to talk about sex and share stories with each other. It can be a confusing topic that raises a lot of questions when we're young, and it's really helpful to hear about other trans people's experiences so we can begin to get a stronger sense of what we would or wouldn't be okay with. The Trans-Heath Conference is a safe space where we can have some very honest conversations that we might not feel comfortable having with our friends back home.

Even my brothers would learn stuff, though they didn't start coming to the conference with Mom and me until they turned fourteen. I remember one year when they were still in elementary school and they heard me saying in the car that I had been playing with some condoms that were being given away at the conference. When Griffen and Sander started laughing and asking how that was even possible, Mom turned around in the front seat and raised an eyebrow.

"Do you boys even know what condoms are?" she asked.

"Yeah, it's what Grandma and Grandpa live in!" Sander answered. My parents cracked up and then set them straight.

During the day at the conference there are about four thousand attendees checking out all sorts of workshops, but a lot of the kids use that time to run around the hotel and nearby Reading Terminal Market, hanging out with each other. There's a special room for tweens and teens to hang out in, but it's never as much fun as exploring on our own.

During Mom's second year there, one of the other moms overheard a hotel worker call us "a bunch of tranny freaks." The parent immediately told the manager what had happened, and she felt so terrible that she organized a small party for the kids in one of the lounge areas, and served ice cream and snacks and drinks. Everyone had such a good time that Mom decided to throw an end-of-conference party every year for the kids—no small feat, since there are usually around two hundred of us—and it's one of the best parts of the weekend. TransKids Purple Rainbow Foundation sponsors it, and the party has grown so big that it now takes up two conference rooms in the basement of the hotel. There's a highly chlorinated indoor pool right next door that the kids jump in and out of as they run between it and the party, which also serves as a meet-and-greet for all the grown-ups to socialize and share experiences.

When we headed back to Philly the summer after seventh grade, there were a lot of kids for me to catch up with. I even ran into Tia from Camp Aranu'tiq! We hadn't really kept in touch, so I wasn't sure if she'd remember me, but she did and invited me to go out shopping with her. I told her I wanted to stay behind but that I'd catch up with her later.

Tia was still really into fashion, and I am not, at least at this point in my life. I can get into shopping for a dress with my mom for big events and special occasions, but I'm mostly happy in my jean cutoffs and a T-shirt. You might not have guessed that if you've seen me on TV, but having cameras follow me around all day absolutely counts as a special occasion.

Anyway, after Tia came back from shopping we got to

finally catch up, and later that night we joined a big group of kids who were hanging out in a hotel room that happened to be parent-free for a while. It didn't take long for someone to break out a bottle for spinning.

When we were all younger, the games at the conference tended to be a lot more innocent—things like Manhunt, which was just hide-and-seek but with teams. When we grew into teenagers, the hormones were flowing and many of us, most definitely including me, didn't have a whole lot of experience.

There were around ten or fifteen of us that night, including the twins, all squeezed into that one hotel room. It wasn't weird for Griffen and Sander to be there, since a lot of the kids bring their siblings. (Plus everyone loved my brothers!)

I don't know what possessed me to announce this, but I blurted, "Maybe I'll finally get to make out with somebody!"

The bottle only spun around a few times before we abandoned the game to just talk instead. I was bummed that it hadn't landed on me once, but it turned out that my brothers were on the case. Griffen pulled me aside and pointed to a trans guy named Timmy who was sitting on a bed on the other side of the room. I didn't really know him, but we'd been introduced earlier that night.

"That's who you should make out with," Griffen whispered.

"Why?" I asked. Timmy didn't seem like my type, but

I wanted more info. I'm always curious to know more if someone likes me!

"He's a huge fan of yours."

Nope, wasn't going to happen.

I get really uncomfortable around people who know who I am but I have no idea who *they* are. I've never gotten used to it, and it's especially bad if the person is around my own age—somehow that feels even more awkward. I guess it's because the person has already made up their mind about who I am, when they don't really know anything about me at all. I worry that any chance of us getting to truly know each other is shot, because I'll feel like I need to stay this eternally positive role model and can never let my guard down and be vulnerable.

I'm so used to living a regular life at school and at home that it's easy for me to forget there's a public side to me as well, until I do something like read mean comments on my YouTube page or someone approaches me and wants to take a picture. I'm not sure I'll ever fully adjust to that.

I told Griffen to let Timmy down nicely and scanned the room. It had suddenly become very important to me that I make out with somebody *that night*. Not because I was really attracted to anyone there, but because I wanted to be prepared when I met someone I liked and who liked me back.

I sat down in the middle of the room, next to a girl named Bryn. She was a couple of years older than me and I'd been friendly with her for years, but we weren't close or anything. Even though I tend to gravitate toward boys, I'd recently begun to consider myself pansexual. I'd never had an actual crush on a girl, but I don't want to ever close myself off to the idea. I can see myself falling for anyone, regardless of gender or gender identity, as long as I like their personality.

I could appreciate that Bryn was really pretty, but I didn't feel anything romantic for her. She had long black hair and almond-shaped eyes and was taller than me by a good four inches.

Still, I decided to just go for it. "Will you teach me how to make out?" I asked her.

She got really nervous and had a panicked look in her eyes, a mirror image of how I felt even though I was pretending to be brave.

"Sure," she finally agreed.

She leaned in, and before I realized it we were kissing! Too bad she was really aggressive. I almost gagged when I felt her tongue hit the back of my throat, and I pulled away to the sounds of all the kids in the room yelling and whistling.

"Okay, well, thanks!" I said, and got up and sat down with a group of people on the other side of the room.

I replayed in my mind what had just happened and knew I could do better. I decided I wouldn't count it as my first official make-out session. I couldn't even really consider it *practice* because I barely got to do anything—her tongue had taken up all the space!

"Want to try that again?" I heard someone say. I turned around and saw that it was Stephanie, the first girl I'd ever met at the Philly conference, sitting right behind me. I'd never noticed it before, but she and Bryn looked really similar.

Since we'd known each other for so long, I decided it would be no big deal.

"Yeah, but let's go out in the hallway," I said. I thought maybe if there weren't so many people around we'd have a better chance of getting it right.

So much for that—as soon as we left the room together a whole bunch of kids realized what was going on and followed us out to watch. We walked down the hallway a little bit to try to get away from them, right around the corner from the elevators. I figured that way we could hear if anybody was coming and separate before we got busted.

My back was against the wall and we started to make out. Stephanie was less aggressive than Bryn but still kind of all over the place. We never got in sync with each other, and all I could think while it was happening was *This is it? This is the big deal?*

The elevator doors dinged, giving me a good excuse to pull away. "Thanks," I said, and we all ran back into the room and cracked up over the whole thing. It had been pretty ridiculous, but I also feel like it bonded us. All of us were still navigating through the idea of love and sex, and I think we helped strip away a little bit of the mystery that night.

When I finally made my way back to the room I was sharing with my parents a few floors down, I used the key card to get in and noticed right away that all the lights were out. The TV was flickering, though, and I could see that Mom and Dad were asleep in the other bed.

I stood there and watched Mom for a second before reaching out and shaking her shoulder.

"Mom," I whispered. "Mom, wake up."

"Huh?" she said, opening her eyes and looking around, confused. I felt bad—I could tell she'd been dead asleep, not just lightly snoozing.

"I French-kissed for the first time," I said. "Twice. With two different girls."

"What?" She was suddenly wide-awake. "Who?"

"Bryn and Stephanie." I watched her process the information.

"Did you have a good time?" she finally asked.

"It wasn't that great," I said, crawling into bed beside her. "Good night."

Camp Aranu'tiq, a place where kids can be their true selves.

CHAPTER 16

"The only opinion that really affects me is my own opinion of myself because I determine the way I am, not anyone else. If someone says something hurtful to you or makes you feel down on yourself, then you just gotta stay positive and keep moving forward."

Scoring some much-needed romantic experience with making out wasn't the only big thing that happened at the Trans-Health Conference that year. In addition to Tia, I'd reconnected with another friend, a girl named Celeste. We'd first met back when I was twelve and my mom took me to tour the Coca-Cola factory in Atlanta, where we were participating in a conference called Creating Change. Mom wanted me to meet a trans girl who was the daughter of one of her friends from her support network. I hadn't been thrilled at the idea of being set up on what was essentially a playdate at that age, but I liked Celeste a lot. She had the same kind of inappropriate humor as me, which basically means we both thought poop jokes were hilarious.

While we were in Philadelphia, Celeste told me she was going to Camp Aranu'tiq that summer, but to the one on the East Coast. They'd finally changed the timing so I could go without missing school. Tia was going to be there as well, and I decided I had to attend, too.

There were still openings left so I got in, and I couldn't wait to catch up with other people I'd met the last time who were also going to the East Coast camp that year. I was excited to see what they looked like now that we were all older. But who am I kidding—I was also pretty desperate for something romantic to happen. Since I finally had a little bit of experience, I felt like I was ready for anything.

I hung out with Sophie before I left, and she told me she'd had her first kiss already, too. None of my other friends were dating yet, but I was starting to feel nervous about being left behind. The boys at school still flat-out ignored me. If a male friend came up to Casey or Sophie, he would give them a hug hello. At best, I'd get an "Oh, hey, Jazz" or an unenthusiastic high five. I pretended not to care, but in truth it always stung a little in the moment. I was holding out hope that the boys in my class would mature when we hit high school, but I couldn't see any of the guys I knew suddenly evolving into an open-minded person who'd be willing to date me. Despite the fact that I wasn't attracted to any of them, it would have been nice to have someone show at least some interest in me.

The East Coast camp is in New Hampshire (that's all the detail you're going to get about location). I was on the same flight as a younger girl also headed to Aranu'tiq named Cathy, who was very sweet but really hyper. Once we landed and were driving to the camp with the counselor, we stopped at a McDonald's and Cathy ordered and proceeded to eat an entire twenty-piece box of Chicken McNuggets all by herself while I stared at her from the backseat, fascinated that someone as small as her could put away so much food.

Just like my first time at Aranu'tiq, we were the very first kids to arrive, and that was when I found out the camp had not only divided up the bunks by age, but all the activities as well! Luckily Celeste was in my cabin, but I hardly got to see Tia at all, except during one hour of free time when the kids could pick whatever activity they wanted. Tia and Celeste and I always chose the same one so we could hang out together.

One thing none of us could do was swim in the lake. And it wasn't just us—the entire camp was banned from it. To be allowed, we had to pass a swimming test, and every single one of us failed. It was a pretty hard test, though. You had to swim to the opposite shore and back again TWENTY TIMES. It was very deep, so you couldn't touch the bottom, and when it came time for me to take the test all I really remember is tons of snot pouring out of my nose and giving up after only a few laps. I did *not* feel like a mermaid in that moment. More like a congested whale with a harpoon in its side. The counselors ended up sectioning off a small corner of the lake that was really shallow so we could at least splash around on hot days, like toddlers in a wading pool.

On some days our little group, along with a pretty girl from Tia's cabin named Sonya, would skip the free activity hour. We'd go to the empty cafeteria instead and just talk. The subject was usually boys, and I'd had my eye on a couple since the very first day. Around the middle of the week one of them, Jonah, came and sat with us and we all started talking about crushes and past boyfriends or girlfriends.

"There's someone here at camp that I like," Jonah said shyly.

"Who?" everyone said at once, me included.

"It's actually someone here at this table," he said, and my heart started beating faster.

"Is there anybody *you* like?" he asked me.

Here's where it all went downhill, in a very typical middle school way. I figured that since he was asking me directly in front of everyone, there was no way his crush could be me. I mean, that would be too obvious, right? I thought he was just trying to deflect attention away from the person he *really* liked.

Because of that dumb thought process, I decided I needed to go on the defensive, too, and fast. All the other campers were starting to enter the cafeteria for dinner. I picked out a random guy and said, "Oh, the person I like just walked in."

Jonah immediately lost all his confidence and I wondered if maybe I had made a mistake. But it was too late. "No one ever likes me," he mumbled. "I'm so ugly."

"No you're not," I protested. "Come on, tell me who it is that you like and I bet she likes you back. You can whisper it in my ear."

He leaned over, cupped his hand to my ear, and whispered, "Sonya."

I stood up to get a tray for dinner. Tia followed right behind me.

"He said he likes Sonya," I moaned.

"I feel like I'm always losing guys to her," Tia said, attempting to sympathize. "Don't worry about it."

"Whatever, I don't care," I said, trying to convince myself.

Jonah and I eventually cleared up the misunderstanding and became sort of a couple. It turned out that he was a younger man, twelve to my thirteen, but he was cute and nice and always said flattering things to me so I thought *Why not?* I think we held hands maybe once or twice over the week of camp. He kept talking about his singing career and how he wanted to be famous, but I didn't pick up on those warning signs until the last day of camp, when Celeste came up to me to say goodbye and told me she had heard Jonah bragging to everyone about how I was going to help promote his music. He thought that since I was kind of a public figure, he'd get a big career boost by dating me. What twelve-year-old is already thinking about things like a "career boost"?!

"I think he's just using you," Celeste said. "I'm sorry."

I was, too. I wish I'd known what he was really after *before* I'd kissed him goodbye behind one of the cabins. Thank God it was just a little pop kiss, with no tongue.

After I got home I ignored Jonah every time I got one of his texts or emails or Facebook messages, and he finally got the hint. Like I've mentioned, I usually shy away from people who think they know me from reading about me or seeing me on TV, but hanging out with Jonah was the first time (that I knew of) that someone had tried to enter my life thinking they could use me to get attention for themselves. I decided I couldn't let that bother me. I wasn't going to let one jerk spoil things and make me scared of dating. Besides, no one in my school really cared one way or another if I was known in the LGBTQ community. And if it ever turned out that someone did have a problem with me, I wouldn't want anything to do with that person anyway.

Since my summer had been sort of a social whirlwind, especially compared to my monklike existence in seventh grade, I decided I was going to try to branch out in eighth grade and make new friends. In addition to hanging out with Sophie again, I reconnected with a few girls I'd been friendly with in sixth grade, and got introduced to a couple more. I made an effort to get closer to girls I already knew who were just casual acquaintances, and for a while I was swinging between two different friend groups, until I decided that was dumb and started having everyone sit together at lunch so we could become one big group. It was pretty easy—I just suggested it, and it happened!

Like any normal middle school friends, we had our arguments for sure. At different times two girls would pair up and make the others feel left out. I got in a huge fight with Sophie one day when I defended someone she was making fun of and said, "Leave her alone. She's a sweet pea."

"Sweet pea?" She cracked up. "Who calls anyone a *sweet pea*? That's so lame!"

At one point the girls accused me of always ruining their fun because I would get so upset anytime one of them made the slightest little joke about someone else in our school. I couldn't stand to hear anyone be made fun of. I'd been working so hard for equal rights my entire life, and in my mind that didn't stop with the LGBTQ community. I believed everyone deserved to be treated with respect. It got so bad that I wrote them all a group text, telling them I couldn't be their friend anymore.

> *I've decided that we are done. You can talk about me all you want to whoever you want, but the inevitable truth is that you treated me like dirt. Even if we did have fun memories and moments (which were undeniably real for me), in the end all you ever did was make me feel bad about myself. But I kept holding on because I had faith that you guys were amazing and would treat me better. But you continued to make*

me feel bad about myself. Friends are supposed to make you feel good about yourself, not bad. I believe in spreading love, not hate. So therefore I say goodbye as a final goodbye. We were going to be best friends forever, but I don't think that ever existed in the first place.

It was all very, very dramatic, and thankfully we made up pretty fast. (And to be fair to my friends, I should confess that I have edited out several swear words that were in the original version of that text!)

I Am Jazz has given us the chance to show that even though I'm transgender, we're still a funny, loving family like so many others.

When I was eleven, I spoke publicly with Barbara Walters again, five years after our first interview. Sharing our story on national TV has helped many other families like ours to find acceptance.

I was so honored to win the Colin Higgins Youth Courage Award when I was eleven. When I accepted the award in New York, I got to ride with the other winners in the New York City Pride Parade.

My acceptance speech at the Trevor Awards. This was my first time speaking before an audience of a thousand people.

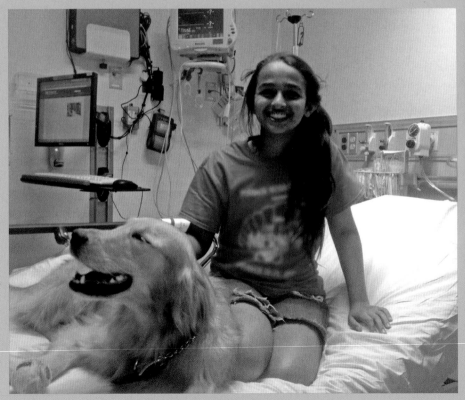

At the hospital getting my new hormone blocker implant. It wasn't so bad thanks to a furry visitor keeping me company.

There wasn't much small talk, but it was cool meeting former President Clinton and his lovely daughter, Chelsea, at the GLAAD Awards.

Katniss!!! I mean, Jennifer Lawrence! She was so sweet and said that she was nothing like her character in real life.

I love drawing eyes.

My siblings are the best! They always have my back.

I was so happy I could participate in the NOH8 campaign. I stand against bullying every day.

When I met President Obama, his aides stressed that we wouldn't have time to talk to him—just shake hands, smile for a photo, and move on. I'm so glad President Obama broke the "no talking" rule.

I never met Oprah when OWN did a documentary about our family. But when she featured me on her show *Where Are They Now?* I finally got to meet the person who had a big impact on my life.

MY MERMAID

My first mermaid costume, age three or four.

I've been drawing mermaids since I was three.

ART BY JAZZ, age 10

This pretty mermaid on a rock shows that my technique has improved—a little.

EVOLUTION

On the beach with my butterfly tail, age thirteen.

Modeling one of my first homemade mermaid tails, age nine.

Being underwater with my mermaid tail makes me feel completely free.

I was so honored to receive the Trevor Youth Innovator Honor.
I hope to continue my advocacy work for years to come.

CHAPTER 17

"Don't be afraid to step out of the shadows, because you are not alone. Be true to yourselves, and live authentic lives in the gender you identify with. I want people to understand that we are just like everyone else."

About six weeks after eighth grade started, *Time* magazine named me one of the 25 Most Influential Teens of 2014.

I sat here for a while trying to figure out how to write that sentence, and decided that being direct was the way to go. It still doesn't feel real. (Even though it happened *again*, just this past year!) With all the media stuff I'd done, I'd been able to keep the spotlight at a healthy distance from my real life and not let it affect me. The *Time* honor hit particularly hard, though. Not because it was about *me*, but because of the company I was in. The thought that anyone would include me on a list with Malala Yousafzai blew my mind. She's one of my idols! When I found out, I couldn't stop jumping up and down. Flattered doesn't even begin to describe the feeling, and my parents were out of their minds with excitement.

Not long after that, I received the Florida Voice of Equality Award, the highest honor given out by Equality Florida, a statewide LGBTQ civil rights organization. It's often given to politicians, and I was the youngest person to ever receive it. It meant so much because it was an award on my home turf! I had to give a speech, and since it was a local ceremony I got to bring some of my friends along with me. It was the first time they had ever seen the public version of me, and having them there made me feel much more relaxed than normal. I felt like I could be goofier and funnier in front of the crowd because my friends were there. That's not to say I didn't take it seriously, and because the award was coming from my state, it was the first time I ever mentioned my home's location in a media appearance.

The accolades were starting to feel like too much, though. Inside, I still wasn't sure if I felt worthy of these huge honors. All I did was talk about love and acceptance, and isn't that just what being human is about? Why was what I had to say so special? Did speaking out even make a difference? Would things ever actually get better?

But when I start to think like that, I remember that shining a spotlight on transgender acceptance is important because it saves lives. I remember the messages and letters I get from transgender kids who have learned to accept themselves because they've seen me being able to live a normal, authentic life, proud of who I am. That's everyone's birthright, yet so many are denied it. If I can remind them to love themselves and stay strong, I'm not going to stop talking.

Reaffirming those things in my mind made it an easy decision to sign up for Clean & Clear's "See the Real Me" video campaign when they approached our family. There were already people like Demi Lovato and the band Fifth Harmony attached, and the marketing department hired a famous director who'd done music videos for singers like Taylor Swift to come and spend a day shooting with me. They brought in a professional stylist to do my hair, who then had to do it all over again after I got thrown in our pool by Sander!

Having a huge company like Johnson & Johnson get behind my message helps ensure that even more people will hear it. The short video I filmed for them has over four million views on YouTube so far. I'm not saying that to show off—I bring it up because it's historic that a mega-corporation with a product line catering to tweens and teens is willing to advocate for transgender rights. Johnson & Johnson even had me visit their headquarters in New Jersey, where I made another YouTube marketing video for them and played a Q&A game where every answer had to be five words. It was all about things like my "summer must-haves" and how I would describe things like the scent of one of their citrus cleansers. They also sent me to several of their other big corporate locations in the Northeast to talk to their employees about my life and help spread transgender awareness. I think the trip was a good indicator of just how far the country has come since we did our first *20/20* appearance. There were virtually no trans kids visible back then. But right after the show aired, more and more families started to come forward to share their own stories, which eventually led to me promoting soap for Clean & Clear! Life is amazingly weird sometimes.

Increased transgender visibility is also why my family agreed to partner with TLC for a reality show. There had been some talk from Oprah's OWN network about doing one for them, but it never panned out. So the idea was already in the back of our minds when a production company approached us. It just had to be the right people at the right time. When we found out the production company wanted to partner with TLC, we decided to go for it. Our goal wasn't fame or tabloid attention; it was to let the world know how normal (and decidedly *not* tabloid-worthy) we really are. We also knew that TLC wouldn't try to exploit us in any way.

I got used to the cameras being in our faces pretty fast, as long as we were inside our house. But anytime we had to shoot outdoors, I was mortified and so self-conscious about having a group of people follow me around, documenting my every move. I can't stand that kind of attention and thought everyone who saw us was pointing and laughing at me: *Who does she think she is?*

The producers and camera crew couldn't have been

nicer, though, and helped me grow more comfortable. Except when it came to eating. Here's a fun little secret about reality TV: Anytime there's a scene that's happening over a meal, you're not supposed to actually eat! The problem is that the sound of chewing gets picked up by all the microphones and ruins any conversations that are happening. So we'd get these heaping plates of food and then just sort of push it around with our forks. (Grandma Jacky's friends all teased her about how much food was always on her plate, because she usually eats like a bird!) We weren't even allowed to sneak in a few bites when the cameras stopped rolling for a minute if the crew needed to tweak something, because we were told it would have looked like the food had somehow magically disappeared when the camera panned back to anyone. (Yeah, that's called eating!)

We learned fast that whenever we needed to film a lunch or dinner scene, we'd need to *really* eat beforehand!

What made the experience so great was that the people on the production crew were so nice and cool. Mom even said she missed having them around after they finished the two-month shoot. It could get a little tiring on the weekends, but for the most part the hours weren't bad at all. I'm a minor, so they had to stick to taping me no more than three hours on school days because of all the child labor laws. (On nonschool days I could shoot with them for eight hours.) Plus they had their own set of union laws so they always made sure to break for lunch and wouldn't film past a certain amount of time, which definitely led to a lot of days where we had to rush through as many scenes as possible. But everyone had a great sense of humor and stayed calm and collected.

Our house was stuffed with lighting equipment in every room, and anything that wasn't a family photo had to come down off the walls, including artwork by anyone who wasn't a family member! Another funny thing is that they weren't allowed to show any logos or brands on camera, so they'd stick a little piece of black tape over the name of everything from soda to our outside grill. (This is true for any reality show—look closely and you'll notice labels torn off water bottles, or laptop computers with strategically placed stickers to disguise the maker.) To this day, we're still finding bits of black tape on condiments in the fridge, which is usually a good indication that the mayonnaise or mustard is past its expiration date!

Unlike other television shows we'd appeared on, when we're usually all dolled up by professionals, we were responsible for doing our own hair and makeup if we wanted to dress up for any particular moment we were shooting. And when we were in a rush it sometimes led to pretty hilarious overuse of things like bronzer and foundation, which showed up under the bright lights.

One Saturday in the middle of shooting, Mom and I had to take a quick day trip across the country to Los Angeles, because Oprah Winfrey had asked to see me. Since we'd already said no to an interview with her when I was a kid and we hadn't gotten a chance to meet her when we had recorded the show for her network when I was eleven, we dropped everything and hopped on a plane.

She was shooting a "Where Are They Now?" special to catch up with people who had appeared on OWN in the past. After we arrived at her office building, we sat down in an outdoor cafeteria to wait, and at the table next to us was a whole group of her employees. We heard one of them mention Caitlyn Jenner and Chaz Bono, so we immediately began eavesdropping. They were talking about how amazing it was that there was now a huge push for transgender rights and visibility, and it felt really good to confirm that Oprah had such an open-minded staff. Mom and I giggled, since they had no idea they were sitting next to a transgender girl who was about to meet with their boss!

When we finally saw Oprah in person, I immediately got why she's such a cultural icon. She radiates empathy and intelligence, and the first thing Mom did was collapse into her arms and give her a big hug! We recorded our interview and I caught Oprah up on everything that was going on in my life. After it was over she told me, "I've done thousands of interviews, but you're a special one. You did a great job." I just about died from happiness! Her praise means so much to me because I admire the way she has used the spotlight and her position to help so many people, which is what I try to do in my own way.

We returned home that same night and continued work on the TLC show. Getting to film with my friends brought us even closer, despite any minor drama that ended up in the final cut. We all had so much fun, which we needed after having our big fight earlier in the year. The final edit of *I Am Jazz* ended up running ten episodes, with one extra as a family "tell-all" at the end of the season, a sort of G-rated version of those *Real Housewives* reunions. I think TLC did a great job of accurately portraying everyone involved, and I hope letting viewers into our home has brought more ideas of acceptance into their homes. We're shooting a second season of the show, so stay tuned!

Word of advice: use the restroom before you
get on line to meet the president!

CHAPTER 18

"I'm just an average person living my life authentically and embracing the fact that I'm transgender. I really hope it will open up people's minds."

Here's a tip if you ever have a chance to meet the president: Pee first!

I had no idea that my family and I would get to meet Barack Obama when we were invited to Washington, DC, for the White House's Pride Month celebration in June 2015. We also had a meeting scheduled with Discovery Communications (TLC's parent company) about the TV show that same morning.

It definitely didn't start out as an auspicious day—our flight the night before had been delayed so we didn't arrive at our hotel until 1 a.m. Of course they had overbooked it, so Mom, Dad, and I tried not to fall asleep standing up while the desk guy frantically called other hotels in the city to find us a room.

By the time we got to the new place, way across town from both buildings we needed to be at the next day, it was 3:30 in the morning. There was only one bed, so we all piled in and conked out. Two hours later the jackhammers outside our window began. The hotel was doing major renovations, and when I stumbled into the bathroom I saw that there was scaffolding outside the window right next to the toilet. I turned the handle on the shades to close them and was sitting there peeing when I happened to glance up and see a man staring down at me through the cracks in the blinds!

I screamed and ran out of the bathroom, but the guy was gone by the time Dad barged in to yell at him. Hopefully he had just been climbing up to work and had been as startled as I was, especially if he happened to see my D!

We thought our meeting with Discovery that morning was just that—a meeting. But it turned out we were being introduced to the entire company to talk about the show, sort of like a meet-and-greet. We were exhausted, delirious, and totally unprepared. To make it more intimidating, the group interview was being broadcast to all of their international headquarters! But everyone from the company was so nice that it ended up being really fun. I was hoping we'd have time for a quick nap before going to the White House, when Mom got an email and started to read aloud

in a panicked voice, "'The President requests your pres-
ence . . .'"

The only thing I cared about at that point was trying
to get an extra ten minutes of sleep, but we had to be at a
specific room in the White House at exactly 4:45 to meet
with President Obama face to face. We changed into appropriate clothes and made the trek all the way back to
the other side of town—and then my heart sank when I
saw the security line that snaked out of the screening area
entrance. It was backed up almost to the end of the block,
worse than an airport on the day before Thanksgiving. It
was already 4:30 when Mom's phone started buzzing and I
heard her say, "We're stuck outside." By the time we got to
the security area, there was someone from the press office
waiting to whisk us inside, but first we had to not just pass
through a metal detector, but also get the once-over from
a bomb-sniffing dog!

It was at this point that I realized how badly I needed
to pee, but I was led into a room and asked to record a short
video talking about the importance of marriage equality,
since it was looking more and more likely that the Supreme
Court was about to make same-sex marriage legal in all
states. Mom tried to tell them that I was scheduled to meet
the president, but we were told, "Oh, don't worry, you'll
still have time."

Having to record the video was a total surprise to me,
but I was able to form some coherent thoughts on the fly,

which came down to the fact that everyone deserves love. As soon as I was done I started to ask if I could use the bathroom, but we were hustled into another room. This one had a line of twenty-seven people who the president had asked to meet personally. We had to hand over our cell phones and were given strict instructions not to stop or say anything to him. We were supposed to walk up, shake his hand, get our photo taken, and leave. At that point I was ready to bail because I thought I was about to have an accident, but a White House aide came over and said, "Oh, you're Jazz Jennings. You're first." We got escorted to the front of the line and I was so relieved. We could get this over and done with quickly and I could find a bathroom.

Only, the president didn't show up. Five minutes passed. Ten, fifteen . . . I was hopping up and down and starting to sweat when suddenly a door burst open and the president came in. We were brought right over to where he was standing.

Don't talk. Shake his hand. Smile, I thought. *You can do this. Then you're out of here.*

"Hello, Jazz!" President Obama said. "Thanks for coming! What grade are you in?"

"I'll be starting ninth grade this year," I managed to answer.

"Really! My daughter is the same age as you."

Don't pee. Don't pee. Don't pee.

Thankfully the photographer interrupted and asked us to smile. He took our picture and the man running the show waved us away, saying, "Okay, you gotta go, we have to hurry this along."

I was ready to bolt, and as I started to turn away I heard the president say, "I'm proud of ya."

It was a once-in-a-lifetime moment, and all I could think was *I'm proud I didn't pee on your carpet!*

In case you were wondering, the White House guest bathroom is pretty impressive. There's a parlor area lined with portraits of former First Ladies, and all the hand towels have the White House insignia on them! Thankfully, I didn't have to wait on line to use the bathroom. . . .

After the president finished meeting with everyone, he gave a speech about LGBT rights, and in the middle of it, I heard a woman start yelling at him. He continued to talk but someone had to escort her out of the room because she kept interrupting him. I was so confused. I'd never even heard the word "heckler" before. I found out later that she had been protesting the treatment of transgender immigrants who have been detained because they are undocumented.

I thought it was nice enough that Barack Obama was inviting the LGBTQ community to his house for this reception, and I didn't think she should disrespect him, especially after all the support he's shown for the community. Her message was definitely valid—the latest number from the US Department of Justice reported that almost 40 percent of transgender inmates are sexually assaulted—but I didn't think she delivered it the right way, especially on such a day of celebration. Sure, there is always more work to be done when it comes to activism and advocacy, but I also think that a party should just be a party, and insulting the host isn't going to help a cause.

As we were leaving at the end of the day, we passed through a glass corridor that had a view of the White House's back lawn. Dad and I spied two people walking close together, deep in conversation, and he joked that it was probably Barack Obama and Joe Biden. As they got a little closer we realized it was! I love the idea that right before a historic moment for gay rights the two of them snuck off alone to talk. I like to think that they, like me (and unlike the heckler), just wanted a quiet moment to take it all in.

My friends are so supportive and so much fun!

CHAPTER 19

"If we come together and get past our differences, then our world will begin evolving from black-and-white and we'll transition into a beautiful place of colors—a rainbow of love, peace, freedom, and equality."

After visiting the White House, much of that summer before I started high school was spent traveling around the country promoting *I Am Jazz*, including a twelve-day trip to Los Angeles with the whole family. At the TLC headquarters there we did the same sort of meet-and-greet with the employees as we had in Washington, DC. The press team set up all sorts of interviews for us with entertainment news outlets like *The Insider*, E!, and *Good Day LA*, and a reporter from BuzzFeed even shadowed us for a few days. The show's PR team gave me a few pointers on how to talk to the media, but I'd already been doing it for so long at that point that it was pretty much second nature.

The strangest moment from that trip by far was walking

with my parents and siblings down Rodeo Drive and having a camera guy from TMZ recognize me. He followed us, shooting and asking questions, just like they do with movie stars! I made sure I was very gracious and talked with him, instead of trying to hide my face behind a shopping bag or punching him out or anything.

We got to use the LA trip as a family vacation, too—it wasn't all work. We visited a theme park called Six Flags Magic Mountain, climbed up to the Griffith Observatory, and went to the Santa Monica Pier. (Of course, it rained for the first time in four months on the one day we got to go to the beach!) One of the executives at TLC even hooked us up with VIP tickets to my family's favorite show, *Big Brother*. We always watch it together at home, and we got prime seats in the studio audience, then stayed behind after everyone left. We met Julie Chen and toured the whole set! We didn't want to leave, and security practically had to drag us out of there.

I Am Jazz premiered during the same trip, but we missed it because we'd been invited to attend the ESPYs, the ESPN awards ceremony where Caitlyn Jenner accepted the Arthur Ashe Courage Award.

Caitlyn has done so much for trans visibility. Since she's part of the Kardashian clan and a historical sports figure, she has been able to share her story on a global scale, not to mention speak to an older generation of people who sometimes have a tougher time grasping what it means to be transgender. Her speech at the ESPYs was moving and inspirational, but what I loved most about it was that she used the opportunity to speak multiple times about how important it is to support trans youth.

When we left the auditorium that night, we stepped into a big open-air plaza and tried to decide what to do next. Mom had gotten a text earlier from a producer on the *I Am Jazz* crew inviting us to celebrate the premiere with them at a restaurant that had a big TV, but we'd already missed the showtime. Mom punched the address into her phone's GPS, and it turned out that the restaurant was right near us! We wandered around in a huge circle trying to find it, until we ended up back outside the auditorium doors and realized it had been right across from them the whole time. We ran over and got to party with all our friends from production after all!

Whenever we weren't traveling that summer and the show was airing a new episode, we'd host a viewing party at our house with friends and family. I thought it would be weird to watch my life unfold on TV, but it wasn't—I'd already lived those experiences, so what was the big deal about seeing them again?

Okay, fine. That's not entirely true. There were a couple of times when I ran from the room crying because I didn't like the way I looked. But it only happened on days when I was feeling extra emotional.

The real problem was that "feeling extra emotional" started happening more and more often, and by the time high school started, I knew my depression had returned.

We adjusted my dosage of antidepressants, and I began seeing a therapist to try to get it back under control.

On the TV show, I talked a lot about how starting high school was going to be a major thing for me, that it would present all sorts of challenges around dating. The idea had definitely been making me nervous, especially since, despite my best efforts, I still didn't have a whole lot of experience in that arena. But as each new episode aired and the school year approached, fears about dating took a backseat to my concerns that the academics were going to be harder than what I was used to. I'd seen the workload all my older siblings juggled with their extracurricular activities, and I got kind of freaked out about how I would handle that much homework on top of soccer and my advocacy efforts. I also grew worried about whether people might treat me differently after I'd been on TV all summer.

Thankfully, things didn't change too much. At the start of the year I noticed that at soccer matches in other towns some people would stare at me for an uncomfortably long time, or I'd run into someone I'd gone to elementary school with and they'd want to take a selfie with me. It was funny to watch girls I barely knew post pictures that I happened to be in with them—and that had been taken years ago—on social media and tell people to "Watch my good friend Jazz's show!" Sam, the guy who'd once called me a chick with a dick, started hanging around me a lot and hinting that he'd love to be on TV with me. Dream on, kid.

It all died down after a few weeks, and everything went

back to normal. Which meant playing soccer, making art, and hanging out with my friends.

It's funny how there are two such extreme sides to my life—what I love about my friends is that they couldn't care less when I do things like meet the president. I mean, they think it's cool, but we don't talk about it after the initial statement of fact. We talk about normal things, like homework and TV shows we love. Sometimes my life feels a little like *Hannah Montana*. One day I'll be on a red carpet with hundreds of cameras flashing in my face, and the next I'm just a regular high school girl taking a math test. On a Sunday, I'll be passing out from exhaustion at a photo shoot while lying on top of a giant mirror, wearing a gown that's more a work of art than clothing, and Monday afternoon I'll be sweating my butt off during a soccer match. I could go on, but I won't, because now I'm starting to worry that this is coming off as conceited. I don't mean it that way. It's just that my life can get pretty crazy sometimes, and I so appreciate that I have a world I can escape back into where everything is normal. Not perfect by any means, but normal.

I'm excited to see what the future will bring.

CHAPTER 20

"Every moment is a new moment for someone to change and become a different person."

It's so weird to think that as you're reading this, you might know more about my life than I do at the time I'm writing this. It will be at least six more months before this book is released, and we're currently shooting the second season of *I Am Jazz*. Anything could happen! How do you end a memoir when you're fifteen? I've only just started out in life, and everything changes so fast. I guess it's a good thing that I *like* changes.

I'm still working on fighting my depression. My friends know all about it, and while they can't really do much, they do the best thing they can, which is to simply be there for me.

Sometimes when I feel the depression start to worsen

and try to drag me down, I can get kind of overly philo-sophical. A whole bunch of dark thoughts will fly through my head, and I have to forcibly talk myself out of them. It's a constant battle, but I think I'm winning.

When I'm at my very lowest, here's where my mind goes: I know I'm not suicidal at all, but in abstract terms I sometimes start to think of what it would be like to not be in this world. Not because of school, or dumb fights with my friends, or the stress of soccer, or being transgender. These are all things I'm fine with. What happens is that I will spiral out into this kind of existential dread that there is no meaning to life, that nothing matters because every-one dies someday and we're all just insignificant specks floating through the great unknown.

Dark, right?

There's a truth I know in my heart, though, that al-ways pulls me out of that place—the meaning of life is the meaning you give it.

Remembering this helps to shut the bad thoughts down. The loving bond I share with my family is what makes life beautiful and worth living. Love is so strong that I just can't ignore its power. Love is what keeps me moving forward.

Want to hear something funny? Aside from a mermaid, there's one other thing I've secretly fantasized about being my entire life—a pirate. Not like an evil pirate—I don't want to go around killing and robbing people. But I'm obsessed with the romance of always searching for a new ocean or a new island. Seeking out adventure anywhere I can find it, not bound by any sort of authority except my own. Pure freedom.

Then I remember that this is exactly what my life will actually be like as soon as I'm out of high school. Maybe I won't have a giant boat and a sword, but I'll be free to pursue anything I want, and the options are endless. There are so many things I want to do that it's almost overwhelming. I could go back to making mermaid tails. I love math and science. I've also gotten really into animation lately, and working with digital art. (Call me, Pixar!) I want to write fantasy books about different realms and fairy tales that interweave to tell a larger story. I want to write a screenplay and learn how to make movies.

No matter what path I choose, I do know one thing. I will never stop fighting for transgender rights. I've learned to cut myself some slack when I get uncomfortable with the media attention. I know I'm not a superhero—I'm an ordinary girl with normal insecurities. I'm incredibly lucky that I've been given a platform to try to inspire other kids to be happy, but that doesn't mean I have to be happy all the time. In fact, I think it would be pretty weird if I were. I'd be like a robot or something. Emotions are what make us able to connect on a very real level. I always tell people to live an authentic life, and being truly authentic means admitting that you can falter. I have my family's unconditional support to pick me back up whenever I do, and I will spend the rest of my life doing everything I can to give other transgender kids that same gift.

MEET JAZZ'S FAMILY

Since my siblings and parents are such an integral part of my life and are a key part of my support system, I thought you might like to hear about many of these events from their perspective. Here are some conversations my editor had with my family.

MEET MY BROTHERS, SANDER AND GRIFFEN

Q: Has it been difficult having your mother travel so much to support Jazz's appearances and events?

S: At times it's tough when your mom isn't there, but my mom does a very good job of balancing her time and making it to as many sporting events and activities as she can. Occasionally she has had to miss some important events, but she has always done a great job of balancing it.

G: No matter what, my mom always finds a way to love us all equally. Yes, she does have to be there to support Jazz more on trips because Jazz is young, so she can't go alone. But my mom always finds a way to show love to all of us.

Q: How often do you all get to travel together for a Jazz-related event?

G: We get to travel quite often. We've gone to awards ceremonies in California and New York, and it's always a fun time. We've been going on more trips in the past four years. When we were younger, we didn't go as much. But sometimes Jazz goes alone with our mom or dad to things like the White House, which we're not always invited to.

S: Yeah, the really cool ones, like meeting the president, we don't usually get invited to. But we have gone to a handful, and it's been a fun experience.

Q: What are your favorite trips?

S: The ESPYs was my favorite. I'm a sports fanatic and I was around all my favorite sports players, so it was pretty cool to escort Jazz down the red carpet.

G: Yeah, the ESPYs was definitely my favorite trip. Jazz let us stay on the red carpet way longer than we were supposed to so we could take pictures of all the athletes. So I thank Jazz for that. It was a pretty cool experience. It was so funny when all the athletes were walking by and Jazz would be like, "Who's that? Who's that?" And we had to explain who all these guys were, and they are some of the most prominent athletes in the world. Jazz had no clue.

Q: Jazz mentioned that you were her mentors for soccer, among other things. Did she have a natural talent for sports? What kinds of things did you do to help her develop her skills and keep her spirits up when she was unable to play soccer with the girls' team?

S: You know our dad is a super athlete—can't you tell? Look how swole he is. He gave us the talent, not our mom, and Jazz has a pretty natural ability to play all sports. Our job was to toughen her up so she wouldn't be a soft soccer player, so she'd be the toughest girl out there.

G: Didn't work.

S: Didn't exactly work because she's still kind of soft sometimes on the soccer field. But she's a great player.

Q: Griffen, how about her mood? When she wasn't able to play, how did you keep her spirits up?

G: Sander and I were always there to push Jazz to be stronger and tougher, but then when she wasn't allowed to play on the girls' team anymore, her enthusiasm and competitiveness dropped a little bit. We just had to keep pushing her and telling her how good she was. Encouraging her and telling her "Oh, you're as good as us" to make her play harder. And I really don't know if she ever fully regained her competitiveness from when she was younger after she wasn't allowed to play on the girls' team. Now she just plays for fun, but she used to be more competitive. She would talk about how she wanted to be a professional, but she doesn't talk about that anymore.

Q: Were you ever at the same school as Jazz? If so, did you ever have to come to her defense in school?

S: Jazz has been in our school in elementary school and high school. There haven't been many instances where we've had to come to her defense. But obviously, if there ever have been any small situations, we've always been there for her. We've explained things to people and gotten them to stop saying false rumors and stuff like that.

Q: Is there a specific instance where that has happened?

G: Most of the bullying toward Jazz hasn't been in school. We've had some social media bullying, which we've always defended Jazz against. We are always there to help her if she needs us.

S: Yeah, like one time this kid said something mean about Jazz on Twitter. So I just said, "Happy birthday to my little sister." He commented back and said "Brother." So then I went to the school and showed it to the dean of discipline. They talked to the kid and he got in trouble, and he never bothered Jazz or me again.

Q: Have you ever lost a friendship over disagreements or negative reactions toward Jazz? Have any of your friends said anything hurtful to you about Jazz?

G: We've never really lost a friend if they found out about Jazz. Not all of our friends are 100 percent accepting. They don't really care about the issue that much, but we've never really lost a friend over it. Our friends have accidentally said things that have been hurtful, but they never do it on purpose. It might be a joke or something that they don't understand offends us.

Q: How do most of your friends react to Jazz?

S: Most of our friends look at Jazz as our little sister. They don't think much of it.

G: They love her. They admire her a lot.

Q: Why do you think most of your friends are accepting of the issue?

G: They think Jazz is pretty special. Not because she's transgender, but because she *is* special. She has a lot of talents; she's just a great person. So my friends embrace that and they understand that and they love her.

Q: Do you think it has helped them to understand what being transgender is?

G: 100 percent.

Q: Jazz has also turned to you for dating advice. You really are amazing older brothers. Do you feel uncomfortable giving that kind of advice to your younger sister, or is this something that has brought you closer?

S: Most of the time it really isn't awkward because my advice to Jazz stays the same: "Stay away from guys. They'll hurt you. And no guy is worth your time at this point." And if there's ever a guy who Jazz likes, I'll look into him and ask her, "Jazz, is this guy really your type?" or "Oh, Jazz, this is a good kid. Maybe you should see what happens." But for now my dating advice to her is stay away from guys.

G: My advice to Jazz with dating is "For now, don't," because I've experienced Sander and Ari both in many troubled dating situations. I've actually never had a really serious girlfriend.

S: LOSER! [laughs]

G: But Sander and Ari both have, and I've seen them both hurt numerous times, crying, things like that. So my advice to Jazz is to stay away for now. She's got too much going for her to worry about a guy. However, if someone came along who was really special, who really liked her for who she is, I wouldn't be against it.

S: She should talk to boys and be friends with boys, but at the same time be careful, because boys want one thing.

Q: Have any of your girlfriends bonded with Jazz, or have any girls given you a hard time because of Jazz's public persona? How has being reality show stars affected your dating life?

G: Jazz doesn't really associate with our friends that much. She is friendly with a couple of our guy friends who are around all the time, but because we don't have any really close girl friends who we hang out with every day, she hasn't had a chance to bond with them. But a lot of them like her, and I think she likes some of them.

S: Retweet. [laughs] It hasn't affected my dating life.

G: It has affected mine to an extent. But I think the main reason it has affected mine is because my confidence has been boosted since the show came out. Like what kid my age doesn't gain confidence from getting 20,000-plus followers on Instagram in a couple of months? That's just the way life is these days for some reason. I don't know if it's wrong, but my confidence is boosted, so from there I was more able to get girls.

Q: When are you leaving for college?

S & G: June/July/August-ish.

Q: What college are you thinking of attending?

G: We're thinking of going to the University of Florida, if we get in, which we find out in a couple of weeks. But I'm also looking at schools like Duke University, Northwestern, Florida State University, and the University of Miami.

S: I have the same answer except I didn't apply to Northwestern.

Q: What do you think it will be like for Jazz to be the only child left at home?

S: Jazz is gonna be yelled at a lot more.

G: Jazz is gonna get really bored without us around the house, I'm sure of that one.

Q: How do you think it will impact your relationship with Jazz and your parents?

S: I don't know. Only time will tell.

G: I've never been away from my house for more than a week on a school trip or something. So I really don't know what it's going to be like. But I hope to stay close with all my family members, and I'll be Facetiming them up in college for sure.

Q: Even though you're twins, you seem to have very different personalities. Do people treat you differently?

S: We are sometimes treated as one person because we're twins, and it really bothers me because he's his own person and I'm my own person. We each deserve to be treated as our own person.

G: For example, our school yearbook has superlatives ["best looking," "most popular"], and there was a superlative we won together. Only one guy and one girl are supposed to win each, but they put us together so we both won the same superlative. And I just thought, well, that sounds about right. We're twins, so they're putting us together and treating us like one person. And it gets annoying.

Q: Did you have any idea your baby brother was really a girl inside before your parents told you?

G: We were really young at the time, so we didn't know what was going on. I just remember thinking things were weird because Jazz would always hang out with Ari playing with the Barbies and not as much with us. I can't remember specifically thinking, "Oh, Jazz is definitely a girl."

S: Yeah, I was really young, so I just remember thinking it was going to change the balance in the family. There were four guys and two girls, but now we were going to have three and three, so it made me sad.

Q: What kind of changes did you see in Jazz after she was allowed to transition publicly?

S: We don't remember.

G: Jazz was just happier after her transition. She's been a happier person. I remember going to her dance recital when she was in pre-K.

S: You don't remember. You've just seen videos.

G: No, I was there. I know I was there. I was taken out of school to be there. I remember that.

S: I don't.

G: Yeah, she didn't dance. Our videos confirm that. But I remember being there.

Q: What are your memories of Jazz filming the Barbara Walters interviews? How did it feel when these shows were on TV? Did your friends or classmates say anything about them to you?

S: I remember Griffen and I didn't take it too well when she was six because we didn't understand. We just thought, "Oh, we're going on TV. We're cool." But then they didn't talk to us and they didn't really interview us. They didn't film us that much, so we were like, "Wait, what about us?" And we were getting mad and told Mom and Dad, "This isn't fair."

G: We ran away, didn't we?

S: Then we ran away, and they came back and got us. We thought it was all about us, and we were just selfish little kids. It was all kid talk. So that's one thing I do remember.

Q: Has being on TV prevented you from doing anything in your regular day-to-day life because you had to film? Were you frustrated to miss out on anything?

G: There haven't been any big things we've had to miss due to filming. There have been a couple of times where I was about to go out with some friends and then they said, "No, you can't, we have to film." But there hasn't been anything major that affected my day or life.

S: When I'm committed to something, I like to stay committed. So sometimes when they made me miss a football practice, I would feel bad because I didn't want to let my team down and I wanted to be at practice. But that's about it.

Q: How does it feel to be recognizable now? Do you have fans of your own?

G: We have a fangirl population, definitely.

S: I'm just living life.

Q: What has made you most proud of your sister? She has accomplished so much—does that ever make you feel pressured about your own lives?

G: What impresses me about Jazz is how humble she is. Most people her age who are on TV and in the spotlight are very arrogant and cocky about it, like, "Oh, I got this, do you?" But she's not like that. She just embraces it and goes with the flow, which is pretty admirable.

S: In terms of the second question, as much as I'm sometimes wowed that my little sister has accomplished so much more than me, I'm here to help her. She has that platform, so we're here to help her. It's not that I should be doing more. It's what can I do to help her because she has that platform.

Q: And what about the message she's sharing?

S: Her message is a message I like to share, too. We all help her share that message because she does have the platform and everyone looks up to her.

Q: What do you wish for Jazz in the future?

S: I hope Jazz just stays Jazz—stays her true self and continues what she's doing. Jazz, your smile belongs to you, so don't let anyone ever take that away from you.

G: If Jazz keeps going down the path she is on right now, she will make big changes in the world. So, Jazz, stay strong.

MEET MY SISTER, ARI

Q: What is it like to be away at college and then return home to film the TV show? Is it a hard balancing act?

A: Being away at school is really fun for me. It's a great experience, learning who I am and what I want to do with my life. Coming back home to film can be a little hard to adjust to because everyone has been dealing with it for the whole time and I have to just jump right in. But it's pretty easy because my family is very comforting. They make it easier for me because they are so good at what they do.

Q: What was that like when Jazz visited you at college?

A: It was interesting. I think she realized how much I enjoy being there, because it's such a cool place to be and it's so diverse. She realized that college is very different from high school, and I think she's looking forward to going to college one day.

Q: Are you still performing and singing? What was it like having Jazz perform with you last year while the show was filming?

A: I don't really perform and sing anymore, but I hope to get back into it because it's something I am passionate about. When I sang with Jazz, it was so fun because I don't normally do that. She's always singing around the house, so it was nice to have her join me. I'm a little shyer about my voice, so it was really fun to sing with her.

Q: What was it like having Jazz at drama camp with you? What was Jazz's most memorable theatrical performance?

A: I think the performance I remember the most was *Cinderella*. I was the fairy godmother, and she was a mouse. I just remember she had a little line or something, and she was really cute. I was so much older, so I would obviously get bigger roles than her, but she was always really talented. At some point I feel like because of her being transgender, people wouldn't give her certain roles. But we all knew she was very talented, and we told her that.

Q: Do you share Jazz's talent for art and drawing? Is this something you do together?

A: I like to color. I don't really like to draw because I'm not very good at it. But I will sit down to paint or draw with her anytime because it's very therapeutic for me. I'm just not specifically talented in that area.

Q: When you meet new people now, do they usually know who your sister is? If not, do you make it a point of telling them, or do you wait until you get to know them better before bringing it up?

A: People don't always know who my sister is, and I usually wait until the subject comes up to talk about it because there's no reason to be like, "Hi, I'm Ari, and my sister is transgender." A lot of people don't even know I'm on TV. I don't really just come out saying that I have a transgender sister as soon as I meet people, unless they know and want to talk about it.

Q: Have you encountered prejudiced people at college who have confronted you or made ignorant comments to you about Jazz? If so, how have you responded?

A: I haven't met any prejudiced people in college. Everyone is very open and friendly, and I really enjoy that about college because they understand that there are a lot of different people in this world. But there are people who are a bit ignorant about the topic, and they're like, "Oh, so when did she get her surgery? When did she change?" That's the biggest thing. I always have to correct them on that. But everyone is very interested and wants to know more and is actually proud of her.

Q: I know you said that it was hard to accept that you weren't the only girl in the family when Jazz first transitioned. What kinds of things did you do with each parent when you were the lone girl in the family?

A: When I was the only girl, I was taken shopping more, maybe to the nail salon, girly things like that. But my sister does that stuff with my mom and me now. Little things like that, nothing major.

Q: What's your favorite family girls' day out?

A: I love it when we go shopping or if we just hang out and watch movies and go to lunch and talk about things that we can't really talk about around the boys. We all understand when it comes to emotional girl things.

Q: Did you have any idea that your baby brother was really a girl inside before your parents told you?

A: I didn't know what to think when Jazz was a baby because I was young. And if I ever saw her sad, it would make me sad. So whatever made her happy, I would go for. I didn't really know she was a girl inside, but I knew something was up.

Q: What are your earliest memories about Jazz's transition? Were there things that were difficult for you to deal with? Or was it just the natural course of events to you?

A: I think the earliest thing I remember was when she was in preschool and she would have to wear boy shorts but could wear girly shirts. When I was little and Jazz had to walk around with her half-grown-out hair and a princess shirt on with boy shorts and boy sneakers, people would give such looks. It wouldn't really embarrass me, but it would make me feel upset because I didn't want people looking at my little sister, or little brother at the time, like that. So it was upsetting.

Q: What kind of changes did you see in Jazz after she was allowed to transition publicly?

A: She was just a bundle of joy. She was always singing, happy, dancing around. I think she finally felt free.

Q: And how about before she was able to transition? Was it different?

A: Yeah, I feel like she had more moodiness and sadness. She wouldn't really say much but would keep it inside and just be sad, and draw things about it that would explain why she was so sad.

Q: What's your favorite part about being on the TLC show?

A: I know that when people watch this, it will change their view about transgender people as a whole and show that they are just normal, and that everyone is human. I love when people come up to me and let me know that they were changed by it.

Q: Has being on the show prevented you from doing anything in your regular day-to-day life because you had to film?

A: I know that if I leave school to film I might miss going out with my friends, but it's not really a big deal because I'll be at school for the next couple of years. I haven't missed anything huge, mostly studying at the library or hanging out with friends.

Q: Do people at school ever come up to you and say, "Hey, are you Ari from *I Am Jazz*?"

A: Every once in a while, but not super often. It depends on where I am. I feel like at my college most people know, but they don't say anything.

Q: What has made you proud of your sister?

A: I'm proud that my sister has changed the world in so many ways. The transgender world keeps changing, and rights keep getting better and better. And she's been such a big part of that. I feel good about standing by her side because she needs the support in order to deal with the amount of pressure she has, and we can help her to keep going.

Q: What do you wish for Jazz in the future?

A: I want her to live a happy and successful life, and I think she has so far. I hope she follows her dream and doesn't feel pressured to do anything she doesn't want to do. And just be herself.

Q: What message would you like to give to other transgender children and their families?

A: I would just say to keep loving each other and being there for each other. And always have empathy because that's one of the main things I try to have in life. You need to always think about how someone would feel and just be there for them and love them.

MEET MY MOM, JEANETTE

Q: Over the years, have you noticed a change in the way people respond to the transgender community?

J: Absolutely. When Jazz first transitioned, people didn't know anything at all. You never saw anybody in the news; it was unheard of. Transgender children and people were in the dark. And now I can say it and they're like, I understand, I know, I get it.

Q: Beyond Jazz, who inspires you?

J: All my children inspire me.

Q: Why?

J: They do things that I couldn't possibly ever do. They're athletic, creative, smart, and gifted in so many ways that I'm not. [laughs] I made these little human beings who are so wonderful in so many ways, and they're my greatest joy. They inspire me to want to be better because they're so wonderful.

Q: What message would you like to give to other transgender children and their families?

J: I want the parents to know that they need to check their egos at the door. They might have a vision of what they wanted for their children or what they wanted their child to be. But they have to remember that those are *their* hopes and dreams, and they have to put that aside for what makes their kids happy. That's the most important thing of all, the happiness of their children. So many families can't do that. They can't put that idea aside. For these parents: Always remember the only way love can last a lifetime is if it's unconditional. Love is not determined by the one being loved but rather by the one choosing to love.

And for the children, I just want them to not be afraid to speak out and share with the adults how they feel and express themselves. Come out of their shadows, like Jazz would say, and be true to themselves and love themselves because they're wonderful.

Q: Were there any people in your life who were particularly hard to tell about Jazz's transition? Were any family members more closed-minded, at least at first? Were any friendships adversely impacted?

J: When it comes to family, I'm going to plead the Fifth. [laughs] However, there were certain friends who I thought were going to be accepting, and then they weren't and they kind of faded away. But I was pleasantly surprised by a neighbor who I thought wouldn't be accepting because she was religious. She came to me one day and said how much she loved Sparkles, because that's what Jazz was going by at the time, and that she believes in her heart that God loves all children. She accepted Jazz into her home, and she was very sweet about it, very accepting.

Q: Were there any other people who surprised you by being supportive and accepting from the very beginning?

J: There were some friends who are still my friends today who said, "You are a great parent for what you're doing for Jazz by allowing her to be true to herself, and never question it." I have one friend in particular—Samantha's mom, Lisa—who treated Jazz like one of her own. She was so protective of Jazz and took her places even before she transitioned. Jazz would be dressed very girly and there would be comments from people, and Lisa just stood up for Jazz and loved her. She called Jazz her little Jarbear. Even today she'll say, "How's my Jarbear?" She moved away, which makes me sad. But she had such a positive impact on Jazz's life and mine by being a friend who just got it right from the start. She loved Jazz so much, and still does.

Q: What was the lowest point for you before you fully accepted Jazz's need to transition?

J: The lowest point was finally accepting that we were going to have to transition, that I would no longer have three little boys and one little girl. That my whole family dynamic was going to change. I'm very bad with change, so I had to release that. I had to take off my necklace with my three blue booties and one pink bootie and store it away forever. And store away all the boy clothes. It wasn't like a death, but it was moving to a new chapter in our lives, and I'm really bad about that. So it was hard to change my idea of what our family was.

Q: What have been the best surprises about this journey?

J: The best surprises have been from complete strangers, like when somebody I don't know writes a letter or comes up to us and says, "I think what you're doing is great, and you have helped me and my family so much. My child may not even be alive today if it wasn't for you." There are no words to describe how things like that impact me. It shakes me to the core in a very positive way, knowing that we've made a difference in the lives of so many people. When I was younger, I would always ask, "What's my purpose in life? Why am I here?" And I feel like I'm here to guide these other families and to help them. That's what I'm here to do.

Q: What do you think about the ongoing legal battles being fought by other transgender families and the way their schools and peers have reacted?

J: There are so many courageous families fighting the bathroom battle, taking it into the courts, to high levels, when we were too afraid to take that on because we were just happy that Jazz could go to school as a girl. There's a young man in particular who is going all the way to federal court so that he can use the bathroom in school. And I'm really proud of the families who are willing to come out and use their names and fight the fight, because they'll set a precedent for those who come after them. I think there are a lot of courageous people out there, and I'm very proud of that.

Q: Jeanette, you have had such an effect on so many children's lives through your advocacy and the foundation. Are there any stories that stand out to you? People who have been helped either by you or by Jazz's story?

J: I have had so many people come to me with their stories, but one of the most memorable for me is a woman who called me many years ago after she got my number from a support group. She just needed to tell me that she knew for a fact that her son would not be here today if it had not been for Jazz. We cried together on the phone and ended up forming a very close bond. Now she's one of my best friends. Her name is Mary. We've talked about her in the book. She just always makes me feel good and has gone on to become a wonderful advocate. So is her son, Chris, who is a lovely young man. Knowing that we impacted the lives of these two beautiful people who mean so much to me and I love so much is a great story in my heart.

Q: What things did Jazz do or say that let you know that allowing her to transition was the right decision?

J: When Jazz was around seven, she went to acting camp. She came home one day beaming. I asked, "What's going on?" And she said, "Mommy, everyone had to go around in a circle and say what their best day ever was, and I wasn't afraid. I came out and told everybody my best day ever was the first day that I was allowed to leave the house in a dress." She shared this very personal thing in front of everybody, and I just thought, "Wow! What a courageous little kid, to say that." Even though she had transitioned, she didn't know who in the group was aware that she was trans, and she didn't care. She just wanted everybody to know that it was her best day ever. I had to fight back the tears.

Q: What do you wish for Jazz in the future?

J: As with all my children, I want Jazz to be happy. I want her life to be filled with unconditional love and joy and very little hardship. Jazz already knows that she can do anything she wants and be anyone she wants. I'd like her to always know that she should reach for the stars, and instead of telling others about her dreams, show them.

Q: Can you say something about Jazz that touches you the most?

J: Jazz touches me in so many ways, but I just love when she laughs. Jazz has this wonderful, wonderful laugh, and it's contagious. And it's such a hearty, beautiful laugh. It makes me happy when I see her happy. It just brings me the greatest joy.

MEET MY DAD, GREG

Q: Were there people who surprised you with how supportive and accepting they were?

G: I can think of one specific instance when I was at the field where the kids played flag football, soccer, and other sports. I remember there was another dad who was a coach, and we often coached against each other. He had a couple of sons and a daughter, and I knew that my boys were close with his sons and Jazz was beginning to get friendly with his daughter. At that time, I know that Sander and Griffen had already slept over at their house a few times. On this one particular day his daughter invited Jazz to sleep over, and Jazz was very excited about the opportunity. But I felt like, "Oh goodness, I don't know if the family knows about Jazz's situation." Usually Jeanette was the person who spoke to the parents in scenarios like this, but I went up to him and asked if he knew about our family and Jazz's story. Surprisingly, as soon as I said it, he said, "Yeah, I know. It's no big deal. We're more than happy to have her over." I just remember letting out a great sigh of relief. It was probably one of the first times that I had to confront an issue like that.

Q: Were any family members more closed-minded, at least at first? Were there people in your lives who were particularly hard to tell about Jazz's transition, or were any friendships adversely impacted?

G: In terms of family, everybody takes things at their own pace as it relates to this issue. You know, I consider my immediate family pretty open-minded. Obviously this wasn't an issue we had ever confronted before. But they were very open-minded about it. I think they were concerned, though. They had the same concerns we had, fears about safety—not just for Jazz, but for the family in general.

It seemed like family members who had some medical background had a more difficult time with the issue, because medical research when Jazz was transitioning wasn't there to back up her experience—the scientific data just wasn't there. So that was a little difficult. I also remember my mom speaking about the issue to an extended family member who had some expertise in psychology and mental health. That person basically told my mom that there is no such thing as a transgender child, and I think that deeply impacted my mom and was hard for her to get over. The issue was not so much how we raised Jazz—I think everyone wanted to support us in making the decisions we made and getting her medical help and treatment. But I think the bigger issue became when we decided to share Jazz's story with the world—not everybody was initially on board with that.

Q: What were the lowest points for you in this experience before you fully accepted Jazz's issue and her need to transition?

G: When Jazz was first diagnosed with gender identity disorder at the age of three, fear was the biggest and first obstacle that I had to hurdle. I had to think about how our family, friends, community, and society as a whole would perceive and respond to Jazz, and to us as a family. I recognized that this was a really complex issue and very little was known about it. And I thought there would be daunting challenges ahead.

Q: What have been the best surprises about this journey?

G: My short answer is the amazing reach of Jazz's story. Jazz is such a remarkable young lady, and her story is a great human-interest story. But what is really surprising and what makes us proudest is her ability to share her story and make it make sense to almost anybody that hears it. She opens the hearts and minds of people throughout the world.

Q: You've made an enormous contribution to the lives of so many LGBTQ children and families through your legal fights to open up the playing field, literally, for Jazz. Have you heard from other families about the difference you've made? Do you have a favorite story like this?

G: I really appreciate the question, and all I can say is I didn't do it for accolades or awards. I hear stories of children getting to utilize the policies that were put in place. As parents and as a family, we have been recognized and honored, and I truly appreciate that. But the bottom line was this was a situation where my child loved to play a sport and she was being denied the right to do something that she loved. And when she was denied, I promised her that I would do everything within my power to change things so she could play. Along the way, I recognized that we had an opportunity to make a difference not just for Jazz but for anyone who might come down the road after

Jazz. I think that's really the spirit of a lot of the things we do. We see an obstacle, and if we can fight the fight, we're doing it for Jazz *and* paving the way for others who maybe won't have to endure some of the hardships Jazz does.

Q: What do you think about the ongoing legal battles being fought by other transgender families and the way their schools and peers have reacted?

G: Things have progressed in this regard. I think as more information about transgender individuals becomes available and more of these individuals have family support, particularly parental support, their families are demanding inclusion and acceptance. We are seeing a change. Maybe it takes a little time, but across the country at local, state, and federal levels, things are getting better. There's a recognized need to include transgender individuals in sports and other institutions. I think it's important to note that in Jazz's soccer fight, the state denied her the ability to play on a girls' team. And part of the reason was that there wasn't an inclusive policy at the national level. But as soon as I got in touch with the United States Soccer Federation and alerted them to the situation, they took unprecedented action to get a policy in place and get Jazz back on the field. I wish all institutions would look to the United States Soccer Federation for guidance, because they did a tremendous job.

Q: What were the hardest moments in these legal battles? I'm sure you kept a lot of it from Jazz's notice since she was so young and the fight went on for so long. I'd love to hear about this from your perspective.

G: I think the hardest part was how frustrating and painful it was to have a statewide organization refuse to open their hearts and minds to Jazz's situation. We gave them tons of information about transgender children, including expert opinions. We linked them to media projects we had done. We gave them position papers, policies used by other organizations, even doctors' letters specific to Jazz, and they just were not hearing it. It was incredibly frustrating. I had written a letter directly to the president of the state organization. It was a heartfelt plea to let Jazz play, and the response was incredibly cold and harsh. I essentially said that the state governing body and their decision to not let Jazz play had taken away a piece of her heart and ours, and I respectfully asked for them to restore it. The board's response was: "Sir, while we understand the concern about your child, the board's position in this matter is unchanged." And that was signed by their president. Dealing with things like that, you feel like you can't win and you don't know which direction to turn. But that's why I went to a higher governing body. I knew at that point that there was no way we were going to win at the state level. Unfortunately, this is not the only such story. Advocating on behalf of a transgender child can be an uphill battle. It's such a struggle for kids like Jazz to be treated equally. But again, I think things are changing rapidly. We lend our hand to these battles, whether it is Jazz, or Jeanette and me, or anyone in our family, as often as we can.

Q: Have you ever regretted your decision to be so public about your family's journey? If so, when and why?

G: This question is interesting. I really don't regret sharing our family story. I think it's made a big difference. It's been a difficult journey, though. None of the media projects that we've ever done happened without a great deal of thought before we decided to embark on the collaboration. We've always been concerned about protecting Jazz and her privacy. But Jazz is not alone in this world, and we wanted to share that a family can get through something like this, and we wanted to make sure other people knew they weren't alone. And one way to do it is to invite people into our home to see Jazz being herself and our family rallying around her and just being a normal, average American family with a unique circumstance. But I also think that every family has unique circumstances. We just happen to be open enough to share our story in the hopes of making a positive change. But it's a balance. We've tried very hard to give Jazz and her siblings a balanced life where they can live like every other teenager and grow up and do things that everybody else does and not have the spotlight on them all the time. A lot of requests come in for Jazz, and as parents we have to vet these projects and make sure that she is able to maintain some ordinariness in her life. But we are also trying to allow her to share her story so it reaches as many people as possible and things change for transgender individuals as quickly as possible. So it's a balance. All the projects Jazz has participated in have been great, but sometimes there are a few too many, so we just slow it down.

Q: What message would you like to give to other transgender children and their families?

G: I think the most important thing for a family to do is to get as much information, learn as much as possible, seek the proper medical opinions, and use your parental instincts to do what you think is right. And just love and support your child unconditionally. Also know that you're not alone, that there are thousands of families in the United States and throughout the world who are in this situation. Find support, go on the Internet, reach out. And don't be afraid.

Q: What do you wish for Jazz in the future?

G: What I wish for Jazz is what most people hope for their children—that Jazz continues to be happy and do things she enjoys and is able to strike a balance between her personal life and her advocacy, if she desires to do that. I hope she keeps going on whatever path she chooses. She has the world ahead of her, and she's done so much at such a young age. I just want her to be happy.

A LETTER FROM GRANDPA JACK

Dear Jazz,

I was there when you emerged into the world less than a few seconds old, when your grandmother said, "It's a boy!" I was there when, as a three-year-old boy, you clearly preferred to wear pink. I was there when your mom allowed you to enjoy your fifth birthday party in a girly bathing suit. I was there when Barbara Walters hugged and kissed you goodbye after spending the day with you, wondering how this pretty little six-year-old demanded to be treated like a girl despite the reminder between your legs. Little did I know that you had more than enough strength to take on nature's practical joke. As you grew older, I realized you had the strength to slam nature's curveball right out of the park. Now as a teenager, I'm watching you give advice to others on your YouTube channel with much more wisdom than any teenager is entitled to have.

I'm not entirely certain where your divine wisdom comes from. As your grandfather, I know life is full of booby traps. Even if I told you to tread softly, how can a grandfather tell a granddaughter which fork in the road to take? I have great confidence that your God-given radar will always take you to a safe haven.

Love,
Grandpa Jack

A LETTER FROM GRANDMA JACKY

"My momma always said, 'Life was like a box of chocolates . . . you never know what you're gonna get.'"—Forrest Gump

This is particularly true in life, where people don't arrive with labels conveniently provided, as with gourmet candies. Having attended the birth of my last grandchild, a healthy baby boy, we were delighted with the adorable addition to our family. Four children born in five years . . . wow! But the bubble was about to burst. As our little boy developed, so did many strange happenings. After the age of two or three, behavior appropriate for a boy was gradually being replaced by feminine actions, eventually leading to the diagnosis of gender dysphoria.

As a grandmother, this threw me into shock and depression. Where do we go from here? My sheltered background, as a result of being raised in the 1950s, never put me in contact with gay or transgender people. What little knowledge I had came from reading novels, biographies, or articles about Christine Jorgensen and Renée Richards, not from experience with people in my world.

Now faced with this situation, I turned to a psychotherapist, who crash-coursed me into the twenty-first century. As Jazz was discovering her world, I had to run to catch up with her. Instead of Grandma teaching the child, the reverse was happening. My daughter, Jeanette, embraced these changes with speed, but not without pain. I followed Jazz and her immediate family, learning the rules while embracing them with love. Among my peers, there was no one to turn to. There were no other grandparents experiencing what we were dealing with. The ultimate challenge came when Jeanette and I attended the annual LGBT conference in Philadelphia. Could Grandma Jacky meet and greet and accept the challenge? Within ten minutes, the answer was a resounding YES! Tolerance, acceptance, and love are what it's all about. Everyone needs that. Doors are opening as some people are hearing the message.

My wish for Jazz is that she will be in a kinder place with what she is accomplishing. With love, hope, and prayers, the journey goes on.

x o x o,
Grandma Jacky

RESOURCES

If you want to do more research on the transgender experience, or are struggling with your own gender identity, there is a gold mine of websites, organizations, and support networks out there. Unfortunately, there's also a lot of misinformation, so here are just a few resources that my family, our friends, and I have all found incredibly useful. (Plus all the websites listed here have their *own* resources sections, which makes it easy to find more information on something very specific, like different types of surgery or hormone replacement therapy options.) I also added some places that will help with depression and suicidal thoughts, along with a list of great books, movies, and TV shows to check out.

WEBSITES

Camp Aranu'tiq
My favorite camp! As mentioned in the book, it's a safe space for trans and gender nonconforming kids to experience all the joys of the summer camp experience in a totally safe environment. **camparanutiq.org**

Gender Spectrum
A fantastic support site with online forums for both teens and parents. The organization hosts a few different conferences about trans youth throughout the year. **genderspectrum.org**

GLAAD

Using the power of all forms of media, GLAAD (Gay & Lesbian Alliance Against Defamation) helps spread the message of LGBTQ support and acceptance on a massive scale. They're the ones that help lead many of the national conversations that happen about LGBTQ rights. **glaad.org**

GLSEN Harsh Realities Report

This is an incredibly important in-depth look into the transgender youth experience in American schools. The report was put together by the Gay, Lesbian & Straight Education Network and shows just how rampant transphobia is in our school systems. **glsen.org**
glsen.org/sites/default/files/Harsh%20Realities.pdf

Lambda Legal

This is our country's oldest and largest legal organization devoted to civil rights for LGBTQ people. They advocate for public policy and select cases to represent that they think will have the biggest impact on our community. **lambdalegal.org**

National Center for Lesbian Rights

NCLR is the awesome group that was so instrumental in helping us with our fight for my right to play soccer. They're dedicated to advancing equality for all LGBTQ people and their families through advocacy and collaboration with other organizations. **nclrights.org**

National Center for Transgender Equality

They're a national legal organization dedicated to advancing civil rights for all LGBTQ people and their families. **transequality.org**

Parents of Transgender Children Facebook Group

My mom is the moderator of this closed group for parents of trans kids. You have to send a request to join because it helps keep out the creeps, but once you're in it's a very loving and safe space. **facebook.com/groups/108151199217727**

PFLAG

Parents, Families and Friends of Lesbians and Gays has a comprehensive online guide for parents of transgender kids, and they do an excellent job of breaking down their resources into very specific needs, like finding support groups for trans women of color. **pflag.org**

Philadelphia Trans-Health Conference

Hopefully you're pretty familiar with this by now! Visit their site to learn more about their mission statement, conference dates, and how to register. **mazzonicenter.org**

TransActive Gender Center

They're a drop-in center located in Portland, Oregon, but they offer fantastic advocacy assistance nationwide. One of their coolest programs is their In a Bind service, which provides binders for trans-masculine youth free of charge. **transactiveonline.org**

Trans*Athlete

A fantastic resource for transgender athletes that includes a state-by-state guide to existing inclusion policies, plus instructions on how to get the ball rolling if you live somewhere without one. **transathlete.com**

TransBucket

If you have questions about surgery and hormone options, this is the place to go. Not only are there detailed descriptions of everything available out there, but there is also a photo-sharing community so people can see the actual results from different doctors. (Be warned—there is a lot of nudity, so make sure you're in a safe space when you register and log on.) TransBucket's own resources section is a wealth of information on almost every topic imaginable that relates to anyone who is trans or gender nonconforming. **transbucket.com**

TransFamily
This is a support group based in Cleveland. It was the very first LISTSERV that my mom reached out to for help, and the discussion threads she joined were her original lifeline when it came to figuring out what was best for me as a child. **beta.transfamily.org**

Transgender Law and Policy Institute
This advocacy group works on law and policy initiatives to advance transgender equality. It's a good site to reach out to if you're trying to find out how certain laws affect the area you live in. **transgenderlaw.org**

TransKids Purple Rainbow Foundation
You've already read a lot in this book about the foundation my family started, but check it out for yourself! You can see many of my interviews, including links to the Barbara Walters specials, as well as read stories about other trans youth and find a pretty extensive list of resources. There is also information about ways you can make a donation to the different programs we support. **transkidspurplerainbow.org**

Trans-Parenting
If you're a parent raising a transgender youth (or even a doctor or therapist working with one), this group provides great educational materials. **trans-parenting.com**

Trans Youth Equality Foundation

Their mission statement says it best: "The Trans Youth Equality Foundation provides education, advocacy, and support for transgender and gender nonconforming children and youth and their families. Our mission is to share information about the unique needs of this community, partnering with families, educators, and service providers to help foster a healthy, caring, and safe environment for all transgender children." **transyouthequality.org**

TransYouth Family Allies

TYFA partners with communities and schools to create supportive environments, and their site has really popular support forums. **imatyfa.org**

DEPRESSION OUTREACH SERVICES

GLBT National Help Center

A great hotline where you can talk to peers about everything from relationship problems to bullying. **glbthotline.org**

Trans Lifeline

A relatively new suicide hotline for and run by transgender people of all ages. In their first year alone they answered over 8,000 calls and trained 300 volunteer operators. **translifeline.org**

The Trevor Project

This is the number one organization for LGBTQ youth suicide prevention. If you are ever having dark thoughts and need someone to talk to, you can call, chat live, or even text with one of their expertly trained staff members. It's such an incredibly important resource, and I'm so grateful that it exists. **thetrevorproject.org**

NOTE:
If you are worried about a suicidal friend or family member, visit the Warning Signs page on the Trevor Project website: **thetrevorproject.org/pages/the-warning-signs**

BOOKS FOR KIDS

10,000 Dresses **by Marcus Ewert,**
published by Triangle Square, 2008
A kid named Bailey dreams about different beautiful dresses every night, and finally finds an older friend who helps make them a reality.

Be Who You Are! **by Jennifer Carr,**
published by AuthorHouse, 2010
Like my picture book, this one is based on a real kid's experience of transitioning at a young age.

George **by Alex Gino, published by Scholastic, 2015**
A very sweet novel about a fourth-grade girl stuck in a boy's body—she *really* wants to play Charlotte in the school production of *Charlotte's Web*.

Gracefully Grayson **by Ami Polonsky,**
published by Disney-Hyperion, 2014
Another book that uses a school play as an important plot device—a sixth grader named Grayson is becoming more and more aware that she is transgender and decides to audition for the role of Persephone.

I Am Jazz by Jessica Herthel and Jazz Jennings,
with pictures by Shelagh McNicholas,
published by Dial Books for Young Readers, 2014
C'mon, you know I had to include it!

It's Okay to Be Different by Todd Parr,
published by Little, Brown Books for Young Readers, 2009
An adorable, brightly colored picture book about all the reasons
why it's—you guessed it!—okay to be different.

Jacob's New Dress by Sarah and Ian Hoffman,
published by Albert Whitman & Company, 2014
This picture book about a kid who prefers to dress like a princess when playing dress-up features not just a supportive family, but an understanding teacher who helps other children get that there's nothing wrong with wearing what you want.

My Princess Boy by Cheryl Kilodavis, published by Aladdin, 2010
The author's child inspired this picture book about a kid who follows his own path instead of any of the gender roles set by society. Who says a boy can't wear a sparkly dress while climbing trees?

When Kayla Was Kyle by Amy Fabrikant,
published by Avid Readers Publishing Group, 2013
One more great picture book about a transgender child, with an emphasis on how much bullying can hurt.

BOOKS FOR TEENS AND ADULTS

Allies & Angels: A Memoir of Our Family's Transition
by Terri and Vince Cook,
published by Hallowed Birch Publishing, 2013
This beautiful and moving memoir is about parents who help their teenage son transition to his authentic self after a suicide attempt.

Becoming Nicole: The Transformation of an American Family
by Amy Ellis Nutt, published by Random House, 2015
The fascinating true story of identical twins, one of whom transitions from male to female. I can really relate to how strong, loving, and supportive their family is.

Beyond Magenta: Transgender Teens Speak Out by Susan Kuklin,
published by Candlewick Press, 2014
Six different trans and gender nonconforming teens tell their true stories. I think it's so important to hear as many different stories as possible to get a real sense of the range of experiences out there.

The Gender Quest Workbook: A Guide for Teens and
Young Adults Exploring Gender Identity by Rylan Jay Testa,
published by Instant Help, 2015
An actual workbook (but a fun one!) that helps guide teens through all the struggles that come along with exploring gender identity.

Hello, Cruel World: 101 Alternatives to Suicide for Teens, Freaks,
and Other Outlaws by Kate Bornstein,
published by Seven Stories Press, 2006
A wild book filled with so much incredible philosophy about gender identity as well as depression. I know this statement is totally contradictory, but it's required reading for rebels everywhere.

Luna by Julie Anne Peters,
published by Little, Brown Books for Young Readers, 2004
Late at night, hidden in the basement, teenage Liam transforms into her authentic self using dresses and makeup. It's a really touching novel about a girl building the courage to reveal her true self to the world. It was a finalist for the National Book Award in 2004!

Mom, I Need to Be a Girl by Just Evelyn,
published by Walter Trook Publishing, 1998
Trailblazer alert! This memoir by a single mom of a transgender teenage girl is a beautiful story of how they navigated the transition together in a pre-Internet world. Some information may be outdated, but the personal experiences recounted in this book are invaluable.

Raising Ryland: Our Story of Parenting a Transgender Child with No Strings Attached by Hillary Whittington,
published by William Morrow, 2015
A really powerful memoir about a family who spent four years teaching their child to speak, because of hearing loss. Once Ryland finally learned to talk, he was able to let his parents know that he was a boy trapped in a girl's body!

Redefining Realness: My Path to Womanhood, Identity, Love & So Much More by Janet Mock, published by Atria, 2014
Janet Mock is a trans activist, journalist, and role model. Her memoir tells about growing up as a child into the incredibly inspiring woman she is today.

Rethinking Normal: A Memoir in Transition by Katie Rain Hill, and
*Some Assembly Required: The Not-So-Secret Life of a Transgender
Teen* by Arin Andrews, both published by Simon & Schuster Books
for Young Readers, 2014

These two memoirs come from a male-to-female and female-to-male teenage transgender former couple. Each book details their early lives and transitions, as well as the story of their dating experience and eventual breakup. They provide different perspectives and explain a lot of the issues that can come up with sex and dating as a transgender teenager.

EDUCATIONAL BOOKS FOR PARENTS OF A TRANSGENDER CHILD

*Gender Born, Gender Made: Raising Healthy Gender-Nonconforming
Children* by Diane Ehrensaft, published by The Experiment, 2011
This guidebook for raising healthy gender nonconforming kids is great because it shows just how wide the spectrum of gender identity really is.

Helping Your Transgender Teen: A Guide for Parents
by Irwin Krieger, published by Genderwise Press, 2011
Written by a clinical social worker, this guide helps parents understand a lot of the thoughts and feelings transgender teens experience.

The Transgender Child: A Handbook for Families and Professionals
by Stephanie Brill and Rachel Pepper,
published by Cleis Press, 2008
This is a comprehensive guide for parents that would have really helped mine a lot if it had been around when I was little.

If you want more book suggestions, search goodreads.com /list for "booklist for trans teens." There are over 200 reader-recommended novels and memoirs about transgender youth, and it's easy to scroll through and find the perfect one for you or your transgender kid.

MOVIES/TV

One of my biggest hopes for the future is that we'll start seeing more transgender actors portraying transgender characters in films and on television. Right now, they're pretty rare.

About Ray (2015)
As of the printing of this book, the movie hasn't been released yet, but it played on the festival circuit in 2015, and I was even hired by *Entertainment Tonight* as a special correspondent to interview the cast on the red carpet at the Toronto Film Festival! It stars Elle Fanning as a female-to-male transgender teen navigating his transition, and his family's response.

Boy Meets Girl (2014)
Yay, a movie with a transgender actress playing a young transgender woman! Michelle Hendley stars in this romantic comedy about relationships in a small town in Kentucky.

Boys Don't Cry (1999)
Anyone who doesn't cry while watching this fictionalized true story of female-to-male Brandon Teena, who was brutally murdered in 1993, is made of stronger stuff than me.

A Girl Like Me: The Gwen Araujo Story (2006)
Lifetime aired this biopic about the devastating murder of Gwen Araujo, who was beaten and strangled by four men after they found out she was trans.

Ma Vie en Rose (1997)
When I was little, I adored this French-language (subtitled, of course) Belgian movie about a very young transgender child struggling to become her authentic self.

Orange Is the New Black
Transgender actress Laverne Cox is brilliant as Sophia on this Netflix comedy/drama about women in prison. It makes for excellent binge watching, but is definitely for older viewers.

Tomboy (2011)
Another French-language (subtitled) film about a transgender child, only this one is about a ten-year-old kid's female-to-male experience.

Trans (2012)
An incredible documentary about the lives of several inspiring people. What I love about this movie is that it shows the transgender experience among several different age groups, from children to people who transitioned much later in life

Transparent
This Amazon show (again, for older kids out there) is titled after a male-to-female transgender parent, but it's really about her entire hysterically dysfunctional family. I appreciate that they cast several trans actors as supporting characters—now let's just make one of them a lead!

ACKNOWLEDGMENTS

I am the luckiest kid in the world to have been blessed with supportive parents, who I'm grateful for every day. They showered me with unconditional love and support while many other kids like me were not so lucky. Thanks for listening to me from the beginning.

I'd like to thank my wonderful siblings. Ari, thanks for always allowing me to raid your closet and steal your toys. I could have never expressed myself without your great taste. And I couldn't ask for more awesome brothers. Thanks, Griffen and Sander, for accepting me from the start and for protecting me forever. I love you all so much.

Thanks, Grandma Jacky and Grandpa Jack, for all your love and for helping my parents when times were rough, and for your contribution to this book. Thank you, Nana Phyllis, Eduard, Grandpa Marvin and Grandma Joyce, for loving and embracing me.

I'd like to thank all my aunts, uncles, cousins, and extended family for making me feel accepted when the rest of the world didn't understand. A special shout-out to cousin Debbie for guiding my parents at times when they may have felt lost.

There are so many friends I'm grateful for. Thanks to you all for holding my hand while others laughed and whispered. Thanks, Samantha and Lisa B., for seeing me as a girl way before many others. To my best friend forever (and guardian angel) Casey, thanks for sticking by my side and bringing joy into my life, and for understanding me better than I understand myself sometimes.

Thanks, Dr. Marilyn, for giving the best advice in the world to my parents, who followed my lead because of you. I'm also truly grateful for the other doctors who have taken great care of me, Dr. Will Charlton and Dr. Sara Hart-Unger. You've made puberty bearable.

I feel lucky to attend a school that fully accepts me, and I hope that someday all trans youth are treated equally in their schools. I appreciate all the teachers and administrators who have had my back.

Thanks to my coaches who fought for my right to play soccer and all those who have always made me feel welcome on the fields and court.

To Barbara Walters and ABC, I will always be grateful for the platform you gave us to share our story. Thanks to my TLC family for putting us in the living rooms of families worldwide. Thanks, Jessica Herthel, for the gift of *I Am Jazz*.

To NCLR, GLAAD, the Trevor Project, Equality Florida, the Colin Higgins Foundation, HRC, and many other advocacy groups, I can't thank you enough for everything you've done for me and so many other LGBTQ youth. You are all invaluable!

I'd like to send the biggest hugs and gratitude to Josh Lyon. You are a gem like no other.

Many thanks to my amazing editor, Emily Easton, and the wonderful Samantha Gentry for spending tireless hours making this book come to fruition. Do you ever sleep? I'd also like to thank our wonderful book agent, Joe Veltre, for finding a home for my story.

To those who have turned these pages, thanks for welcoming me into your hearts. I hope my story will help others with gender dysphoria, and inspire our allies to pay it forward.

Finally, I'd like to thank all of those who have paved the way for transgender people. Without their courage, the world would be a very different place for kids like me.

CATCHING UP WITH JAZZ

So many things have happened since I finished writing this book! In April 2016, our show, *I Am Jazz*, tied for a GLAAD Media Award with *I Am Cait* for Outstanding Reality Program. I was totally shocked, but somehow pulled off an acceptance speech, which was very intimidating with thousands of eyes on me and celebrities like Demi Lovato and Nick Jonas completely focused on my every word.

June was probably the busiest month in my life. We went to Philly again for the Trans Health Conference. It was tons of fun, but no Spin the Bottle or Truth or Dare this time. As soon as the conference was over, I had to hop on a plane for a week of promotion for the book you are now reading and season two of *I Am Jazz*. It was a whirlwind! During this press tour, I received word about the tragic shootings at the Pulse nightclub in Orlando. The LGBTQ community was shocked and scared. My family actually had to beef up security because we feared for our safety.

At the end of the month, I was so honored to be the youngest Grand Marshal in the New York City Pride parade. This was also the month that my brothers left for college. My mom cried almost the whole way home. That July, I literally binge-watched my favorite shows every day. In August, my whole family, minus Ari (she had a school commitment), traveled to London. It was hands down the best vacation of my life. School started at the end of August, and we began filming season three. Then it was time to celebrate my sweet sixteen. When I was younger, I thought I'd have a big party for my sixteenth birthday, but parties are overrated. So I went to a drag show with my family instead. I LOVE drag queens! Later that night I received the best birthday present in a big box with doughnut wrapping paper. Inside was a tiny kitten, who I named Dunkin, since he came in a doughnut box. He's my new baby.

The following month I went to Orlando Pride. It was so emotional. I rode on a float with one of the Pulse victims. I've never met anyone so brave. It really put life in perspective for me and had a deep impact. In November, I spoke at a Transgender Day of Remembrance memorial. A record number of transgender individuals were murdered in 2016, which is devastating.

After the New Year, we finished filming season three. You'll have to tune in to learn more about my dating situation, and my quest to find a doctor to perform my bottom surgery. Yikes! We filmed the family scuba diving, and I went on Tomi Lahren's conservative show to stand up for transgender people's bathroom rights.

Finally, I have some big news. The Tonner Doll Company has created a Jazz doll. She's eighteen inches tall and the first transgender doll to hit mainstream shelves. I'm excited to watch my little doll break down barriers in a new and fun way.